The Best Dishes from Thailand, Japan,
China and More Made Simple

Vegan Asian
A Cookbook

Jeeca Uy

Creator of The Foodie Takes Flight

PAGE STREET
PUBLISHING CO.

PAGE STREET
PUBLISHING CO.

First published in 2021 by
Page Street Publishing Co.
27 Congress Street, Suite 105
Salem, MA 01970
www.pagestreetpublishing.com

Distributed by Macmillan, sales in Canada by The Canadian Manda Group.

25   24   23   22   4 5

ISBN-13: 978-1-64567-280-7
ISBN-10: 1-64567-280-8

Library of Congress Control Number: 2020948909

Cover and book design by Kylie Alexander for Page Street Publishing Co.
Photography by Jeeca Uy

Printed and bound in the United States

To everyone who believed in me:
Thank you for helping me
spread my wings.

Table of Contents

Introduction

Hello! 你好 nǐ hǎo! Mabuhay!

In case you're reading this with little to no background on me, I'm Jessica, but I usually go by Jeeca to my friends and family. I've been vegan since I was seventeen years old. Back in 2015, I started my food blog and Instagram account The Foodie Takes Flight, where I wanted to document my day-to-day meals and re-create my favorite dishes from growing up. Little did I know that I'd be able to reach hundreds of thousands of people with my food and stories. Back then, I just really wished I had someone to guide me as I navigated my way through cooking and preparing Asian food as a vegan!

I was born and raised in the sunny (and really humid) Southeast Asian country of the Philippines, which comprises over 7,000 islands (depending on whether it's high tide or low tide, ha ha). I grew up in a multilingual household with my parents speaking a mix of English, Filipino and Hokkien. I'm fifth generation Chinese from my father's side—my great-great grandparents emigrated from Fujian province in China and settled down in the Philippines. My upbringing was a mix of both Chinese and Filipino traditions, which greatly influenced my tastes and preferences for cooking. I have vivid early memories in the kitchen, learning tips and tricks from my mother, who herself had learned them from both my guama (my mother's mom) and ama (my father's mom).

I've also been lucky enough to have been exposed to a plethora of cultures, as my parents love to travel. They are the two most hardworking people I know and they strove tirelessly to provide for my sister and me. They wanted to be able to visit a new country and city every year if time and budget permitted, to be able to see more than just the sights but also to give us a better understanding and view of the world. This really paved the way for my love of food and culture that I got to immerse myself in firsthand. These are memories I cherish and hold on to to this day, and I'm immensely grateful for the chance to experience them early on in my childhood.

This cookbook is a compilation of some of my favorite East and Southeast Asian dishes growing up—be it from family gatherings, favorite restaurants, travels or simply from home-cooked meals.

While I love dining out and trying out new dishes, whether it be in a casual Chinese restaurant or in a little hole-in-the-wall ramen alley, there's really nothing like home cooking. I wanted to create recipes that didn't sacrifice flavor for ease and instead wanted to strike that balance of simple yet really flavorful meals you could easily cook at home using easy-to-find ingredients. There are, of course, certain pantry items you'll have to stock up on to be able to really achieve that desired flavor you can't get elsewhere. Once you have those few staples, these recipes are what you can whip up for yourself or your loved ones for a simple weeknight meal or celebration.

Be prepared for a whole chapter of recipes just for tofu because, yes, tofu is probably the building block of Asian cuisine (see what I did there!), especially for vegans, as it's an amazing source of protein. There is also a chapter comprising noodle and rice recipes because both of these are staples in Asian households. In a Chinese-Filipino household, we have an endless supply of rice and noodles, so trust me when I say that we can't live without them. I'll be sharing many different ways you can enjoy your rice and noodles— and you will probably end up having seconds, even thirds.

I wanted the recipes in this book to reflect the cultures of these dishes and do them justice, all while making them as simple and approachable as possible. I've always believed in the power of food to bring people together. I really hope the recipes in this book can take your palate on a little tour across East and Southeast Asia and leave you, your friends, family and other loved ones with happy and satisfied bellies.

Lastly, if there's one thing I learned from my mom in the kitchen, it's to taste as you go and adjust depending on what suits your preference! She never really followed recipes to a T and went with her instincts and taste buds. So, even though these recipes have their respective lists of ingredients and measurements, I want them to serve merely as a guide to determine the overall flavor profile of the dish. Every recipe is very flexible and you'll see a lot of lines stating "adjust depending on your desired taste." So, don't hesitate to do just that and, of course, to enjoy the process of cooking and getting creative in the kitchen.

Happy cooking!

With all my love,

Jeeca

Selecting, Storing and Preparing Tofu

I use tofu as a main ingredient for a lot of the recipes in this book since it is really versatile, high in protein and a great substitute for meat in traditionally meat-based dishes. Not only is tofu commonly used in vegan cooking, but it's also an ingredient that's been ingrained in Asian cuisine for generations. As you probably already know, there are three common types of tofu: silken, firm and extra-firm. In this section, I will share my tips about how to select, store and prepare each type, hopefully to give you a better understanding of each one.

Selecting Tofu

My go-to type of tofu is extra-firm because it's the easiest to store and cook with. It's also the "meatiest" in terms of texture because it's much more compact compared to the other types of tofu. Of course, the type of tofu needed will vary based on the recipe you're making. Firm tofu is best used for deep-frying, as it holds up well enough to be fried into a nice golden crisp with little worry of it breaking apart. You can get it crispy on the outside, while on the inside you still get that juicy bite. Both firm and extra-firm tofu can easily become the main ingredient in a dish, as they're both good replacements for meat because of their texture. You will also find baked or smoked blocks of extra-firm tofu, which are already marinated. These usually have a very light smoky flavor that can go well with stir-fried dishes such as fried rice or noodle dishes. Silken tofu, on the other hand, is much more delicate to work with, but what it brings to a dish is a different experience altogether—it adds a nice smooth and velvety texture to delicious, saucy recipes, such as Mapo Tofu (page 61), that really takes them to a whole new level.

As for where to purchase tofu, if there are local soy or tofu stores or Asian groceries in your area, that would be the best place to check. Tofu in Asian stores can come in Styrofoam trays covered in plastic wrap. If there is a tofu maker where you can purchase freshly made tofu, this is your best option, because there's nothing like fresh tofu! You'll really notice the difference between freshly made tofu and those packaged ones in the refrigerator section of supermarkets or grocery stores.

If your only option is to purchase from supermarkets or grocery stores, try to look for tofu that still has a lot of time left before reaching its "best before" or expiration date. If possible, check its production date. The problem I find with tofu from grocery stores is that it's often sitting in that same container with the same liquid for days, even weeks, and can start to turn sour in smell and taste. If you're also able to see through the plastic packaging, try to look for tofu with clear liquid, as the liquid will start to turn into a thick and somewhat cloudy color when it's been sitting there too long.

Storing Tofu

Silken tofu: Silken tofu can come in block form in sealed containers or in a long tube-like plastic wrapper. I find that the tube type stores better and longer since it's completely vacuum sealed and secure.

Firm and extra-firm tofu: Extra-firm and firm tofu usually come prepackaged in vacuum-sealed plastic trays with some water in it. As mentioned earlier, these pieces of tofu have often been sitting in that same liquid for days or weeks, which can give the tofu an off-putting taste and smell. Additionally, some tofu can turn slimy to the touch when it's been sitting in that same liquid for too long.

If buying a vacuum-sealed package from the grocery store, my tip is to remove the tofu from its packaging, rinse it under running water, transfer it to a large, airtight container and then fill that container with fresh cool water, enough to completely submerge the tofu. Refrigerate the container and replace the water every 2 days until you're ready to use the tofu. My tofu lasts for up to 2 weeks when rinsed and stored in airtight containers. If you find that your tofu has turned slimy when removed from the water, give it a good wash and smell it. If it smells sour and rancid, discard the tofu. But if the tofu smells normal after being rinsed, it's still good to go!

Preparing Tofu

Silken tofu: There is little to no preparation needed for silken tofu because it's very soft and can easily break apart, so you need not wrap it in towels or press it to release excess liquid. The most you can do is transfer it to a tray or other flat surface, slice the pieces as needed for a recipe and carefully dab it with paper towels to absorb some of its excess liquid. If you let the silken tofu sit on a flat surface, you'll notice that it'll release excess water on its own.

Firm and extra-firm tofu: Since the firm types of tofu are much easier to handle, you can wrap them in towels or paper towels to squeeze out the excess liquid. These types of tofu are like sponges and are already holding a significant amount of water when you purchase them. So, it's essential that the water is removed from the tofu to be able to properly season and enjoy it.

How to Press Firm and Extra-Firm Tofu

Wrap your tofu in a paper or kitchen towel, then place it on a plate or any flat surface.

Place two chopping boards or any weighted flat item, such as a plate, on top of the tofu to squeeze out the excess liquid. I usually leave the boards on for a good ten minutes. Just make sure that the boards aren't too heavy, since this can squish and completely break the tofu apart. You'll notice afterward that your tofu has slightly shrunk and lost significant amounts of water that is absorbed by the towel.

An alternative to this towel and board method is to invest in a tofu press—because, yes, one exists!

After the tofu has been drained of its excess liquid, soaking it in a marinade or cooking it in a sauce will make it absorb all that flavor and make it taste so much better.

Freezing Tofu

I know a good number of people who swear by using frozen tofu, as it creates these beautiful layers in between the blocks of tofu, mimicking the meaty texture you'd find in chicken or even pork. This is because tofu is filled with a significant amount of water and, as it freezes, it creates these little pockets, and even layers, and once the water melts down, those layers and pockets remain. Some even go to the extent of double-freezing tofu: freezing the tofu, defrosting it and then freezing it again before thawing and squeezing out the excess liquid.

I find that some tofu doesn't hold together well after being frozen, even if it's of the same firm or extra-firm type as others that do fine. I believe this is from the curdling process done by the manufacturers, so it can be a hit or miss, depending on the tofu you have, and therefore it might take some trial and error at the beginning. The freezing and thawing process is totally worth it, especially for certain recipes, such as the Char Siu Tofu (page 58), Japanese Tofu Tonkatsu (page 66) and Sweet and Spicy Crispy Korean Tofu (page 62), that you can enjoy even more with a "meatier" texture similar to chicken.

If you plan to freeze your tofu for a recipe, slice it into slabs or cubes (depending on your preference or what's needed in the recipe), then place the pieces on a tray or container with a cover and allow them to freeze overnight. You don't need to press your tofu prior to freezing. After the tofu has frozen, simply thaw it at room temperature and then, once completely thawed, carefully squeeze out the water from the tofu. I usually like to do this by hand, simply squeezing out the water with my finger if the tofu previously had been cut into cubes. If I'm squeezing out water from a slab of frozen tofu, I simply place it on my palm and carefully squeeze out the liquid by applying pressure.

Delicious Dim Sum and Dumplings

Dim sum dishes are usually served in small portions to be shared, with bamboo steamers filled with various kinds of dumplings and buns stacked on top of one another, leading to that little suspense and surprise as to which of the little bites you'll get to try first! Dumplings in all shapes and sizes are my personal favorite, and those in this chapter are filled with tofu and vegetables to re-create that satisfying bite. Whether they're steamed, boiled or pan-fried, they're best enjoyed with the various condiments and dipping sauces to add to all the deliciousness. Here, you'll also find other options, such as wontons and fried egg rolls, with their deliciously crisp exterior and hearty filling.

Tofu Wontons in Chili Soy Sauce

These wontons are filled with tofu, carrot and scallions soaked in a deliciously fragrant chili soy sauce. You'll probably find yourself having a plateful, so it's a good thing this recipe makes over a dozen pieces.

Makes 18 wontons
Prep Time: 25 minutes
Cook Time: 15 minutes

18 (3½" [9-cm]) square wonton wrappers

Pinch of salt

TOFU FILLING

14 oz (400 g) extra-firm tofu

5 medium-sized dried or fresh shiitake mushrooms, diced

1 tbsp (15 ml) sesame oil

⅔ cup (35 g) chopped scallions, plus more for garnish (optional)

2 cloves garlic, minced

1 medium-sized carrot, peeled and finely grated

2 tbsp (30 ml) soy sauce, or to taste

¼ tsp ground white pepper

¼ tsp salt, or to taste

¼ tsp Chinese five-spice powder (optional)

2 tbsp (16 g) cornstarch

CHILI SOY SAUCE

½ cup (120 ml) wonton or vegetable broth

1 tbsp (15 ml) chili-garlic oil with sediments, or to taste (homemade recipe on page 157)

1 tbsp (15 ml) soy sauce

1 tbsp (15 ml) rice vinegar

1 tsp cane sugar

1 tsp sesame seeds

1 tsp sesame oil

If using frozen wrappers, let them thaw at room temperature until pliable. Cover with a cloth to prevent them from drying out.

Prepare the tofu filling: Press the tofu (see page 11 for more details). Afterward, place the tofu in a bowl and crumble it with your hands or a fork. If using dried shiitake mushrooms, soak them in boiling hot water in a small bowl, covered, for 15 minutes.

Heat a medium-sized skillet or wok over medium-high heat. Add the sesame oil. Once hot, add the scallions and garlic, then sauté for 2 minutes. Add the carrot and mushrooms. Sauté for 2 minutes, or until tender. Add the crumbled tofu, soy sauce, pepper, salt and five-spice powder (if using). Mix well and then cook for 2 minutes. Add the cornstarch and mix until well incorporated. The cornstarch will help bind the mixture together. The tofu mixture will thicken as the cornstarch dissolves. Turn off the heat, transfer the filling to a large bowl and let cool for at least 5 minutes.

Place 1½ teaspoons (8 g) of the filling in the center of a wonton wrapper and then seal to make a wonton. Continue until all the filling has been used to make a total of 18 wontons. See page 30 for a step-by-step pleating guide for wontons.

Cook the wontons: Bring a large pot of water to a boil over high heat. Add a pinch of salt. Once boiling, lower the heat to medium-high, then add eight to ten wontons, depending on the size of your pot. Boil the wontons for 1 to 2 minutes, moving them around with a spoon to prevent them from sticking to the bottom. Once the wontons float to the top and the wrappers are translucent, use the spoon to scoop out the wontons from the water. Repeat this for the rest. Don't discard the water after cooking, since it can be used as the broth for the sauce.

Prepare the sauce: In a small bowl, mix together the ½ cup (120 ml) of broth and the rest of the sauce ingredients, adjusting according to your desired taste. Pour the sauce over the cooked wontons. Serve garnished with scallions, if desired.

To freeze, place the wrapped, uncooked wontons on a tray. Freeze for 3 to 5 hours, or until hardened, before transferring to a container or bag. Boil the wontons from frozen; no need to thaw.

Steamed Chive and Cabbage Dumplings

There's really nothing like steamed dumplings served hot in a bamboo steamer. These are made with a delicious savory mixture of tofu, chives and cabbage, which gives the filling a nice crunch and added texture. You can also opt to pan-fry these dumplings as potstickers, if you're after those nice crispy, golden brown bottoms. Enjoy these with your favorite dipping sauce or a blend of soy sauce, Chinkiang (Chinese black) vinegar and chili sauce for a kick of spice.

Makes 35 dumplings
Prep Time: 35 minutes
Cook Time: 25 minutes

35 (3" [7.5-cm]) dumpling wrappers (homemade recipe on page 24)

16 oz (450 g) extra-firm tofu

2 tbsp (30 ml) sesame oil

2 cloves garlic, minced

1 oz (30 g) Chinese chives, sliced

3 large scallions, sliced

5 packed cups (500 g) shredded cabbage

2 tbsp (30 ml) soy sauce, or to taste

¾ tsp salt, or to taste

¼ tsp ground white pepper

¼ tsp Chinese five-spice powder (optional)

2½ tbsp (24 g) cornstarch

Sesame seeds, for garnish (optional)

DIPPING SAUCE

3 tbsp (45 ml) soy sauce

1 tbsp (15 ml) Chinkiang (Chinese black) vinegar

1 tsp chili-garlic oil with sediment (homemade recipe on page 157)

EQUIPMENT NEEDED

Bamboo steamer

Parchment paper

If using frozen wrappers, let them thaw at room temperature until pliable. Cover the wrappers with a cloth to prevent them from drying out.

Prepare the filling: Press the tofu for at least 10 minutes to drain the excess liquid (see page 11 for more details). Afterward, place the tofu in a bowl and then crumble it with your hands or a fork.

Heat a large skillet or wok over medium-high heat. Add the sesame oil. When the oil is hot, add the garlic, chives and scallions. Sauté for 2 minutes. Afterward, add the cabbage and tofu. Increase the heat to high. Season with the soy sauce, salt, pepper and five-spice powder (if using). Mix well, then cook for 3 to 4 minutes, or until the cabbage is tender. Lower the heat to medium. Add the cornstarch and mix well. The tofu and cabbage mixture will start to thicken as the moisture from the tofu absorbs the cornstarch. Cook for 2 to 3 more minutes, or until the mixture is very well incorporated. Turn off the heat, then let the filling cool for at least 5 minutes.

While the filling cools, make the dipping sauce: In a small bowl, mix all the ingredients together, adjusting according to your desired taste. Set aside.

Divide the filling into 35 portions. I use a large tablespoon to scoop a generous amount before rolling and compressing it in my palms to create an oval ball of filling.

Place a ball of filling in the center of a wrapper before sealing and pleating. Continue until all 35 balls are sealed within their respective wrappers. See page 28 for a step-by-step pleating guide and storage tips for dumplings.

Now, it's time to prepare your steamer. If using a bamboo steamer, heat a large skillet or wok over high heat with enough water to graze the bottom edges of your steamer. Once the water comes to a rolling boil, lower the heat to medium. If using a steamer with a glass or metal lid, wrap the lid with a large kitchen towel to help

absorb the moisture from the steam. Line your choice of steamer with parchment paper to prevent the dumplings from sticking. Working in batches, place your dumplings on the lined steamer. Ensure that the dumplings are spaced at least ½ inch (1.3 cm) apart from one other, as the dough will expand slightly as it cooks. Steam the dumplings for 10 to 12 minutes, or until the dumpling wrappers turn slightly translucent. Repeat this for the rest of the dumplings as needed, depending on the size of your steamer.

Garnish the dumplings with sesame seeds, if desired. Serve these while still hot, with the dipping sauce.

Potstickers Option

You can opt to pan-fry your dumplings instead of steaming by simply heating a large, nonstick skillet (choose one with a lid) over high heat, then adding 1 tablespoon (15 ml) of neutral oil to coat the surface. Once the pan is hot, add nine dumplings, spaced apart from one another, and cook them, uncovered, over medium-high heat until the bottoms are golden brown and crisp, 5 to 6 minutes. Then, pour in ¼ cup (60 ml) of water. Immediately cover the pan with a lid and steam the dumplings until the water has evaporated and the dumplings are cooked through, about 6 minutes.

Crispy Vegetable Egg Rolls

While we were growing up, fried egg rolls were a favorite among us kids. Whenever we'd attend someone's birthday party or a family gathering in a Chinese restaurant, there were always egg rolls and a sweet chili sauce for my cousins and me. These rolls are filled with a mix of vegetables before being fried to a crisp and then dipped in sauce for a delicious finger food that's perfect for sharing.

Makes 12 rolls
Prep Time: 20 minutes
Cook Time: 30 minutes

12 (8½" [22-cm]) square flour spring roll or lumpia wrappers

VEGETABLE FILLING
2 tbsp (30 ml) neutral oil

½ large onion, diced

2 large scallions, thinly sliced (white and green parts included)

2 cloves garlic, minced

5 packed cups (500 g) shredded cabbage

1 cup (120 g) shredded carrot

1 medium-sized bell pepper, seeded and thinly sliced

2 tbsp (30 ml) water

1 tsp salt, or to taste

1 tbsp (15 ml) soy sauce, or to taste

¼ tsp ground white pepper

1½ tsp (5 g) sesame seeds

TO COOK AND SERVE
Neutral oil, for frying

Sweet chili sauce, for dipping

If using frozen wrappers, let them thaw at room temperature until pliable. Cover the wrappers with a cloth to prevent them from drying out.

Prepare the vegetable filling: Heat a large skillet or wok over medium-high heat. Once hot, add the oil, then sauté the onion, scallions and garlic for 1 minute. Then, add the cabbage, carrot and bell pepper. Add the water to cook down the carrot. Season the vegetables with salt, soy sauce and white pepper. Mix well, then lower the heat to medium and cook for another 3 to 4 minutes, or until cooked through and the water from the vegetables has evaporated. Mix in the sesame seeds. Taste the filling and feel free to adjust the seasoning according to your desired taste. Turn off the heat, then let the filling cool for at least 5 minutes.

Wrap the rolls: Prepare a small bowl of room-temperature water to seal the wrappers. On a flat surface, place a square wrapper, arranging it in such a way that it faces you as a diamond shape. Add 2 tablespoons (20 g) of the filling on the bottom pointed section of the wrapper. Note that the amount of filling will depend on the size of your wrappers.

Fold that bottom section to the top, away from you. From there, using both your index and middle fingers, push down the filling to compress it and slowly fold the wrapper again, until you have reached the middle of the wrapper. Dip your finger into the bowl of water and then dab it on both the left and right pointed sides of the wrapper. Fold both pointed sides toward the center of the wrapper before continuing to roll to the top pointed edge of the wrapper. Dab the topmost pointed edge of the wrapper with some water before rolling toward the edges to properly seal the roll. Repeat this step for the rest of the filling and wrappers.

Cook the rolls: Heat a large skillet over high heat with enough oil to submerge at least the bottom half of the spring rolls. Once the oil is hot and releases small bubbles, add six rolls or more, depending on the size of your pan. The rolls should rapidly sizzle in the oil. Flip the rolls after 2 minutes, or once the first side is golden brown, and cook the other side. Once both sides are golden brown, remove the rolls from the oil. Transfer the rolls to a strainer or a paper towel–lined plate to drain any excess oil. Repeat this for the rest of the rolls. Do not turn off the heat until all the rolls are cooked and have been removed from the pan, to ensure they won't absorb the oil.

Let the rolls cool for a few minutes. Do not cover the rolls, so they stay crispy. Enjoy the rolls while they're hot and dip in your favorite sweet chili sauce.

Baking Option

You can also bake the egg rolls by brushing the rolls with oil before placing them on a parchment-lined baking sheet and baking them in a 400°F (200°C) oven for 40 minutes, flipping halfway through. They will, of course, not turn as evenly golden brown and juicy, but still very crispy!

Baked Wonton Cups with Sweet Chili Tofu

These crispy little wonton cups are filled with tofu coated in a sweet chili sauce. You'll love the crunchy bite from the wonton cup and the saucy, "meaty" texture from the tofu. Of course, you can also get creative with your fillings and add other vegetables of your choice.

Makes 12 wonton cups
Prep Time: 15 minutes
Cook Time: 25 minutes

WONTON CUPS
12 (3½" [9-cm]) square wonton wrappers

Neutral oil, for brushing

SWEET CHILI TOFU
14 oz (400 g) extra-firm tofu

½ tsp salt

Neutral oil, for frying

1 small white onion, diced

1 small red bell pepper, seeded and diced

1 small green bell pepper, seeded and diced

¾ cup (180 ml) your favorite sweet chili sauce, or to taste

1½ tsp (8 ml) soy sauce, or to taste

GARNISHES (OPTIONAL)
Chopped scallion

Toasted sesame seeds

Prepare the wonton cups: If your wrappers were frozen, ensure that they are thawed at room temperature and pliable, or else they can easily tear.

Preheat your oven to 350°F (180°C). Brush a thin layer of oil in each well of a 12-well muffin tin. Carefully press down each wonton wrapper into the well.

Place the muffin tin in the oven and bake until the wonton wrappers are golden brown, about 12 minutes. Remove from the oven and let the tin cool for 5 minutes before removing the wonton cups.

Prepare the tofu: Press the tofu for at least 10 minutes to drain the excess liquid (see page 11 for more details). Afterward, slice it into ½-inch (1.3-cm) cubes. Place the tofu in a bowl and sprinkle with the salt. Carefully mix to coat.

Heat a large skillet over medium-high heat. Add enough oil to cover the surface of the pan. Once the oil starts to bubble, add the tofu. Fry the tofu, moving it around every 2 minutes, until golden brown throughout, about 6 minutes total. Remove the tofu from the oil and then transfer to a strainer to drain any excess oil. Set aside.

Empty the oil from the pan. Over medium heat, sauté the onion until translucent, about 1 minute. Add the bell peppers and sauté for 3 to 4 minutes, or until tender. Add the sweet chili sauce and soy sauce. Mix the sauce well, then simmer for 2 minutes. Add the tofu and let it cook in the sauce for 2 to 3 minutes, or until the sauce thickens. Taste the tofu and then feel free to adjust according to your desired taste by adding more sweet chili sauce or soy sauce, as needed. Turn off the heat and let the tofu cool for 5 minutes.

Assemble the wonton cups by adding 1 to 1½ tablespoons (15 to 20 g) of the filling to each cup. Garnish with chopped scallion and sesame seeds, if desired.

Notes: You can prepare the baked wonton cups a day before and then let them cool completely before storing, unfilled, in an airtight container. You can prepare the filling ahead, too, and simply reheat it in a pan before using. Make sure to store the cups and filling separately until ready to assemble.

Char Siu Tofu Gua Baos

These fluffy steamed buns are filled with sweet and savory char siu tofu with a delicious and refreshing bite from the pickled carrot and cucumber. Finish them off with some chopped peanuts and chili. You can enjoy these as a snack or as a delicious meal in itself.

Makes 12 gua baos
Prep Time: 30 minutes
Cook Time: 15 minutes

PICKLED CUCUMBER AND CARROT

1 cup (280 g) seeded and thinly sliced cucumber

⅔ cup (85 g) thinly sliced carrot

1 tbsp (19 g) coarse salt

¼ cup (60 ml) rice vinegar

1½ tbsp (25 g) cane sugar, or to taste

1 tsp toasted sesame seeds

GUA BAOS

12 steamed buns (homemade recipe on page 26)

1 batch Char Siu Tofu (page 58)

Chopped roasted peanuts

Chopped red chiles (optional)

Prepare the pickled cucumber and carrot: Place the cucumber and carrot in a colander. Place another bowl underneath to catch the liquid. Add the salt and mix it into the carrot and cucumber. Leave the vegetables to sit for at least 10 minutes. Afterward, squeeze out the excess liquid. Rinse the cucumber and carrot under running water to wash off the salt and then squeeze them out to drain any excess liquid.

Meanwhile, in a medium-sized bowl, mix together the rice vinegar, sugar and sesame seeds until the sugar has dissolved. Mix the drained vegetables into the vinegar mixture. Taste and feel free to adjust the measurements according to your desired taste. This can be prepared a day or two in advance, as it gets better when the vegetables soak in the pickling mixture; the pickled vegetables can be refrigerated for up to 1 week.

Prepare your steamer. If using a bamboo steamer, heat a large skillet or wok over high heat with enough water to graze the bottom edges of your steamer. Once the water comes to a rolling boil, lower the heat to medium. If using a steamer with a glass or metal lid, wrap the lid with a large kitchen towel to help absorb the moisture from the steam.

Steam the buns for 8 to 10 minutes, then remove the pan from the heat. Leave the lid on the steamer for 10 minutes before opening and removing the buns from the steamer. Transfer the cooked buns to a tray or plate, then cover them with a clean, damp towel so they don't cool too quickly and dry out.

Assemble the gua baos: Carefully open a steamed bun. Add a piece of char siu tofu and then a generous amount of pickled carrot and cucumber. Add some chopped peanuts and finish off with some red chile, if desired. Repeat to fill the other buns.

Homemade Dumpling Wrappers

Makes 35 (3-inch [7.5-cm]) dumpling wrappers
Prep Time: 60 minutes
Dough Resting Time: 20 minutes

These homemade dumpling wrappers are made with only three ingredients. They're very pliable, which will make it much easier to pleat your dumplings without the need for any extra water.

2½ cups (310 g) all-purpose flour, plus more for dusting

¾ tsp sea salt

¾ cup (180 ml) warm water

Potato starch or cornstarch, for storing wrappers

EQUIPMENT
Rolling pin

Prepare the Dough

In a large bowl, stir together the flour and salt. Create a well in the center of the mixture, then pour in the warm water.

Using a spatula or chopsticks, mix the flour and water together. Once the dough starts to come together, you can use your hands to mix. At this point, you can opt to work in your large bowl for minimal cleanup or transfer the dough to a lightly floured surface. Scrape the dough from the sides of the bowl and knead for 7 to 8 minutes, or until the dough is smooth and doesn't stick to your hands.

Shape the dough into a large ball, then place it in the center of the bowl. Cover it with a clean, damp towel and let it rest for 20 minutes.

Divide the Dough

Flour your work surface by taking a pinch of flour and then spreading it with your palm over the surface. Remove the dough from the bowl and transfer it to your floured surface. Punch your thumb into the center of the dough to create a hole. Slowly pinch and stretch the sides to make a larger hole that will ultimately create a ring about 12 inches (30 cm) in diameter.

Sprinkle the dough with flour. Using a knife, slice the ring of dough into 0.5-oz (15-g) pieces, making about 35 pieces in total.

Place the pieces of dough back in the bowl and cover with a towel to prevent them from drying out.

Roll Out the Wrappers

Lightly flour your work surface. Take a piece of dough and roll it into a ball. Lightly flatten it with your palm.

Sprinkle a little flour on top of the dough and lightly coat your rolling pin with some flour as well. Roll out the dough by moving the rolling pin forward and backward across it. Rotate the dough 90 degrees and then repeat the movement. Continue to roll out the dough until you have a wrapper that is about 4½ inches (11.5 cm) in diameter. If you can't make it into a perfectly round shape, that's totally fine!

Repeat this for the rest of the dough until you have rolled out each ball into a wrapper. Keep the wrappers on a tray covered with a clean, damp towel to prevent them from drying out while you work on each one.

How to Store the Wrappers

Although homemade wrappers are best used when freshly made, if you plan to make them ahead of time, here's how to store them:

Sprinkle about ¼ to ½ teaspoon of potato starch or cornstarch onto each wrapper, then spread the starch around to coat both sides. Repeat this for the next wrapper and then stack it on top of the first wrapper, until all the wrappers are coated with starch and stacked. This is to prevent them from sticking to one another when stacked.

Divide the wrappers into seven stacks of five pieces each. I like to divide the wrappers into smaller stacks so I can work with them by batch. Wrap the dumpling wrappers tightly in plastic wrap and then place them in an airtight container large enough to keep them from bending, before placing them in the refrigerator or freezer.

The wrappers can be kept in the refrigerator for up to 2 days or in the freezer for up to 1 month. To use, let them come to room temperature before carefully separating. Please note that since these wrappers have been coated with starch, you will need water to seal them when using.

Homemade Steamed Buns

Enjoy these homemade fluffy steamed buns with the fillings of your choice. They can be prepared ahead of time and frozen, too.

Makes 12 buns
Prep Time: 40 minutes
Inactive Dough Rising
Time: 60 minutes
Cook Time: 30 minutes

DRY INGREDIENTS
2¼ cups (275 g) all-purpose flour, plus more for dusting

1 tbsp (8 g) cornstarch

¼ tsp salt

YEAST MIXTURE
¾ cup (180 ml) soy milk or other nondairy milk (either unsweetened or sweetened; both work!)

1 tbsp (15 g) cane sugar

1 tsp instant dry yeast

1 tbsp (15 ml) neutral oil, plus more for brushing

EQUIPMENT
Bamboo steamer

Parchment paper

Rolling pin

Prepare the Dough

In a large bowl, mix together the dry ingredients.

Prepare the yeast mixture: In a small, microwave-safe bowl or measuring cup, microwave the soy milk on high for 25 to 30 seconds (note that this can vary depending on your microwave) until the milk is about 110°F (42°C). It should be warm to the touch but not hot enough to burn you. If it's too hot, let it cool for a few minutes.

Mix the sugar and yeast into the warm milk. Let it sit for 10 to 15 minutes, or until it foams. When it's foamy, mix in the oil.

Make a well in the center of the dry ingredients. While mixing with a spatula or chopsticks, pour in the yeast mixture. Keep mixing until a dough has formed. At this point, you can opt to knead it inside the bowl if your bowl is large enough to minimize the mess, or you can place it on a lightly floured surface. Knead for 8 to 10 minutes, or until the dough is smooth.

Scrape off the flour on the sides of the bowl, if necessary. Keep kneading for another 2 to 3 minutes, or until the dough is stretchy and no longer sticks to your hands. The gluten bonds will strengthen as the dough is kneaded. Shape the dough into a ball, then place it in the center of the bowl. Cover it with a clean, damp towel and let it rest in a warm place for at least 1 hour, or until doubled in size.

Form the Buns

Once the dough has risen, transfer it to a lightly floured surface. Punch your thumb into the center to create a hole. Slowly pinch and stretch the sides to make a larger hole that will ultimately create a ring about 10 inches (25 cm) in diameter.

Slice the ring of dough into 12 pieces, each piece weighing about 1.8 oz (50 g).

Place the pieces of dough back in the bowl and then cover with a clean, damp towel to prevent them from drying out while you work on each bun.

Prepare your bamboo steamer and gauge how many buns can fit. An 8-inch (20-cm) bamboo steamer can fit four shaped buns. Only prepare the buns that can fit in your steamer at a time. Line your bamboo steamer with a sheet of parchment paper to prevent the buns from sticking.

Roll a piece of dough into a ball and then lightly flatten it on a floured surface. With a rolling pin, roll the dough until you have an oval that is about 3 x 4½ inches (7.5 x 11.5 cm).

Brush the dough with a thin layer of oil, then fold in half. Transfer the buns to the bamboo basket. Cover the buns and let them proof for another 15 to 20 minutes.

Repeat this step for the rest of the dough, working in batches as needed, depending on how many can fit into your steamer.

Cook the Buns

Heat a large skillet or wok over high heat. Ensure that the pan is large enough to fit the bamboo steamer. Add enough water that it touches the bottom edge and grazes the steamer. Make sure the water doesn't reach the parchment paper and buns.

Place the steamer on the pan. When the water comes to a boil, lower the heat to medium. Steam the buns for 8 to 10 minutes, then turn off the heat. Leave the steamer, covered, on the pan for another 10 minutes before removing the steamer from the pan. This is to prevent the buns from quickly cooling.

Transfer the cooked buns to a tray or plate, then cover them with a dry towel so they don't quickly dry out.

Shape more buns and then leave them to proof in the bamboo basket. Repeat the steps to steam the next batch. Repeat this for the rest for the dough.

How to Store the Buns

Place each bun on a small piece of parchment paper to prevent it from sticking, then place the buns in a freezer-safe container.

You can freeze the buns and reheat them by steaming directly from frozen for 12 minutes, or until cooked throughout.

How to Fold and Store Dumplings

Folding dumplings can be quite tricky at first try, so you can always start with the simplest method—which is to completely seal the wrapper without any pleats. I find that wrapping dumplings work best with homemade wrappers because they're much softer and pliable than store-bought ones. So, if you're using store-bought frozen wrappers, make sure they've been thawed at room temperature and that you have a bowl of water ready to be able to dip your fingers into, to seal the edges.

Lastly, if you're starting out, add less filling to your dumplings so you're able to better seal them. You can always slowly increase the amount of filling as you go along and get more used to the process.

IMPORTANT NOTES

Keep your wrappers covered with a damp towel to prevent them from quickly drying out.

Cover the completed dumplings with a damp towel, too, to prevent them from drying out too quickly.

TO FREEZE DUMPLINGS

Place the wrapped dumplings spaced apart on a freezer-safe tray. Freeze for 5 to 6 hours, or until the dumplings are hard. Afterward, remove the dumplings from the tray and place in freezer-safe bags or containers.

Do not thaw frozen dumplings before cooking them. Cook directly from frozen, to prevent the dumplings from getting soggy and breaking apart.

FOR POTSTICKERS

Place the frozen dumplings on a hot pan in which you have heated some oil over medium heat and cook until a lightly browned crust has formed. Add the water and cover to cook in the steam.

TO STEAM

Prepare your wok to steam the dumplings. Once the water comes to a boil, place the dumplings on your parchment-lined bamboo steamer and steam for 10 to 12 minutes, or until the wrappers have turned slightly translucent.

How to Fold Dumplings

1. Place a wrapper on your hand. If using store-bought wrappers, prepare a small bowl of water and dab some water around the edges of the wrapper.

2. Add a ball of the filling to the center of the wrapper. Compress the filling, if needed.

3. While using your finger to push the filling in, carefully pinch the wrapper to bring the bottom to the point at the top. Then, carefully hold the top of the wrapper with your fingers by pressing both ends together.

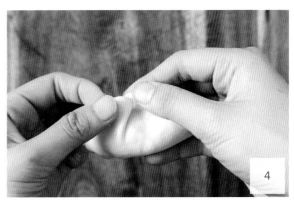

4. Starting on one side of the dumpling, pinch the wrapper nearest the middle to create a pleat toward the center. Press down the pleat.

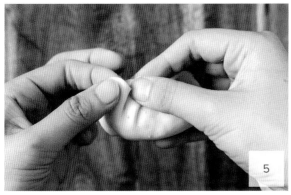

5. Pinch the wrapper again and then create another pleat, toward the center. Repeat this until all the pleats have been completed on one side of the dumpling.

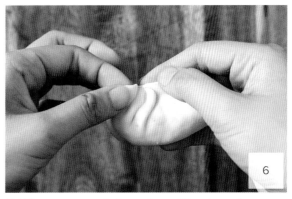

6. When you reach the edge of the dumpling, carefully press down the pointy edge to create that crescent moon shape.

7. Now, repeat this process for the remaining side of the dumpling. Pleat starting from the middle and then fold the pleats toward the center.

8. Press down the pleats to ensure the sides are sealed tight. Repeat the pleating process for the rest of the filling and wrappers.

How to Fold Wontons

1. Prepare a small bowl of water. Carefully separate the wrappers. It's best to work with the wrappers at room temperature so they're pliable and won't easily break. Place a wrapper on a flat surface to appear as a diamond shape with a pointed edge facing you. Dip your finger into the bowl of water and then trace the edges of the wrapper.

2. Add 1½ teaspoons (8 g) of the filling to the center of the wrapper. Compress the filling into a small ball. Note that the amount of filling will depend on the size of your wrapper and the type of fold you're doing.

3. Grab the bottom point of the wrapper.

4. Holding the bottom point of the wrapper, fold it diagonally until you have a triangle. Seal tight and carefully press out the sides of the filling to remove any excess air pockets.

5. Rotate the triangle 180 degrees.

6. Carefully press down the center. Dab a bottom corner of the triangle with a little water.

7. Carefully bring both bottom ends together and then press both ends to seal them together.

8. After shaping and folding each wonton, set aside on a tray and cover with a damp towel to prevent them from drying out. Repeat for the rest of the wrappers and filling.

Flavor-Packed Rice Bowls and Noodle Stir-Fries

This chapter has some of my favorite rice and noodle dishes, reminiscent of my travels and experiences while growing up and made vegan by substituting certain proteins and creating simple homemade sauce alternatives.

You can enjoy Pad Thai (page 46) from the bustling streets of Bangkok: A deliciously sweet and savory homemade sauce coats rice noodles with an added crunch from toasted peanuts, tang from lime and an extra kick of spice from chili. Try an easy Nasi Goreng (page 38) by a roadside warung in Bali—fried rice cooked in a sweet, syrupy soy sauce (kecap manis) and packed with nutrient-rich veggies for a really satisfying meal. You can mix together a bowl of Spicy Dan Dan Noodles (page 54)—a delicious and numbingly spicy Szechuan classic of noodles enveloped in a rich and fragrant sauce, which will leave you asking for more.

If you're looking for something to satisfy your taste buds with a bowl or rice or noodles (or both!), this chapter has flavor-packed recipes that can be easily made and enjoyed as complete meals on their own or cooked with vegetables and tofu.

Thai Pineapple Fried Rice

There's nothing like pineapple fried rice—how well the sweet, juicy pieces of pineapple go with the savory sauce! This also contains cashews for that extra bite and texture, with a hint of spice from the chili. Enjoy this delicious fried rice as is, or paired with your favorite barbecue.

Serves 3
Prep Time: 10 minutes
Cook time: 20 minutes

3 cups (500 g) cooked and cooled rice, leftover is best

14 oz (400 g) extra-firm tofu

3 tbsp (45 ml) neutral oil

½ tsp salt, divided, plus more to taste if needed

1 small onion, diced

½ cup (75 g) seeded and diced red bell pepper

2 tbsp (30 ml) soy sauce

2 tsp (10 g) coconut sugar, or to taste

2 tsp (4 g) curry powder

½ tsp chili powder, or 1 bird's eye chile, sliced (optional)

¼ tsp ground white pepper, or to taste

1 cup (165 g) fresh or canned pineapple chunks, sliced into ½" (1.3-cm) cubes

⅓ cup (45 g) roasted cashews

½ cup (30 g) chopped scallions, plus more for garnishing

½ cup (90 g) seeded and diced tomato

Place the rice in a large bowl and carefully break apart with a spoon to separate the grains. Set aside. If using freshly cooked rice, leave the rice to cool in front of a fan for 10 minutes for the moisture to evaporate.

Press the tofu for at least 10 minutes to drain any excess liquid (see page 11 for more details). Afterward, slice into ½-inch (1.3-cm) cubes.

Heat a large skillet or wok over medium-high heat, then add the oil. Once hot, add the tofu cubes. Sprinkle ¼ teaspoon of the salt over the tofu and then give it a good mix. Pan-fry the tofu cubes, flipping them about every 2 minutes, until golden brown and crisp on all sides, about 10 minutes total. Move the tofu to the side of the pan. Add the onion and bell pepper. Sauté for 2 minutes, or until the bell pepper is tender. Add the rice and then season with the soy sauce, coconut sugar, curry powder and chili powder or fresh chile. Mix well and then season with the remaining ¼ teaspoon of salt and the white pepper.

Add the pineapple and increase the heat to high. Give the mixture a good stir and cook for 2 to 3 minutes, stirring occasionally to prevent the rice from sticking to the bottom of the pan. Add the cashews, scallions and tomato. Mix well and cook for 2 more minutes. Adjust the seasoning according to desired taste, as needed. Turn off the heat and then serve the rice in bowls or pineapple bowls. Garnish the rice with more chopped scallions, if desired. Enjoy while hot!

Shiitake Teriyaki Fried Rice

This is inspired by my favorite Japanese yakimeshi, or fried rice—it's short-grain rice cooked with fresh shiitake mushrooms and homemade teriyaki sauce. I love using short-grain rice because of its higher starch content and stickiness. This fried rice is packed full of umami with a delicious hint of sweetness from the sauce.

Serves 2
Prep Time: 10 minutes
Cook Time: 15 minutes

3 cups (500 g) cooked and cooled short-grain rice, leftover is best

4 oz (115 g) fresh shiitake mushrooms

2 tbsp (30 ml) neutral oil

3 scallions, thinly sliced

1 tsp minced fresh ginger

2 cloves garlic, minced

1 small carrot, peeled and finely diced

1 small red bell pepper, seeded and diced

½ tsp salt, plus more to taste if needed

Splash of water

3 to 4 tbsp (45 to 60 ml) teriyaki sauce (homemade recipe on page 160), plus more to taste if needed

¼ tsp ground white pepper

1 tsp dark soy sauce (optional, for color)

Chopped scallion, for garnish (optional)

Toasted sesame seeds, for garnish (optional)

Place the rice in a large bowl and break apart with a spoon to separate the grains. If using freshly cooked rice, leave the rice to cool in front of a fan for 10 minutes for the moisture to evaporate.

Separate the caps and stems of the shiitake mushrooms. Discard any tough stems if using large mushrooms. Thinly slice the caps and stems into ¼-inch (6-mm) pieces. Set aside.

Heat a large skillet or wok over high heat. Add the oil. Once hot, add the scallions, ginger and garlic. Sauté for 1 minute, or until aromatic. Add the carrot and bell pepper. Sprinkle in the salt and add a splash of water to cook down the carrot. Lower the heat to medium-high heat and cook for 3 minutes, or until the veggies are tender. Increase the heat to high, then add the shiitake mushrooms. Leave the mushrooms untouched for 2 minutes to lightly brown on the bottom and then repeat to lightly brown on the remaining side.

Add the rice to the pan. Cook for 2 minutes, then pour in the teriyaki sauce. Add the white pepper as well. Lower the heat to medium-high and then mix the rice well to coat it evenly with the sauce. Cook for 2 to 3 more minutes. Mix in the dark soy sauce (if using). Taste the rice and then season with more salt or teriyaki sauce, if desired. Turn off the heat.

Scoop the rice into bowls and pack them tight before flipping the bowls over on plates to create a rounded shape. Garnish the rice with chopped scallion and toasted sesame seeds, if desired. This is best enjoyed while hot.

Indonesian Fried Rice (Nasi Goreng)

You only need one pan to whip up this fried rice and enjoy a satisfying blend of sweet, spicy and savory. Nasi goreng is an Indonesian dish; its name literally translates to "fried rice." The secret to this dish is the kecap manis, a sweet, syrupy and dark soy sauce that gives this fried rice its distinct color and caramelizes the rice as it cooks.

Serves 2
Prep Time: 10 minutes
Cook Time: 25 minutes

FRIED RICE

3 cups (500 g) cooked and cooled rice, leftover is best

7 oz (200 g) extra-firm tofu or other vegan protein

2 tbsp (30 ml) neutral oil

1 small onion, diced

4 cloves garlic, minced

2 bird's eye chiles, sliced (adjust according to desired taste)

¼ cup (35 g) frozen peas

⅓ cup (40 g) diced carrot

1 small red bell pepper, diced

3 tbsp (45 ml) sweet soy sauce (kecap manis; homemade recipe on page 161)

Salt and freshly ground black pepper

TO SERVE

Sliced tomatoes

Sliced cucumber

Chopped scallions (optional)

Place the rice in a large bowl and break apart with a spoon to separate the grains. This is most easily done if the rice has been cooled prior to cooking. If using freshly cooked rice, leave the rice to cool in front of a fan for 10 minutes for the moisture to evaporate.

Press the tofu for at least 10 minutes to drain any excess liquid (see page 11 for more details). Afterward, slice into ½-inch (1.3-cm) cubes.

Heat a large nonstick skillet over medium-high heat. Once hot, add the oil. Pan-fry the tofu cubes, flipping about every 2 minutes, until golden brown and crisp on all sides, about 10 minutes total.

Add the onion and sauté until translucent, about 3 minutes. Add the garlic and sliced chiles. Cook for 2 minutes, or until the garlic is lightly browned.

Add the peas, carrot and bell pepper. Sauté until the vegetables are cooked through, about 5 minutes.

Add the rice. Pour in the sweet soy sauce. Mix well. Season the rice with salt and black pepper to taste. Continue to cook for 2 to 3 more minutes. Turn off the heat.

Serve with sliced tomatoes and cucumber and then top with sliced scallions, if desired.

Yang Chow Fried Rice

This dish is always present during family gatherings and celebrations at Chinese restaurants. It's a total hit with everyone, but most especially for the kids. It's a simple yet really tasty fried rice that's usually cooked up with egg, but in this vegan version I used tofu to mimic that texture. The rice is seasoned with a simple mix of black salt, or kala namak, and white pepper to maintain the golden yellow color of the rice.

Serves 3
Prep Time: 10 minutes
Cook Time: 25 minutes

3½ cups (600 g) cooked and cooled white rice, leftover rice is best

TOFU
8 oz (225 g) extra-firm tofu
1 tbsp (15 g) packed cane sugar
1 tbsp (15 ml) soy sauce
¾ tsp ground turmeric
Pinch of black salt (kala namak) or sea salt (see note)

VEGETABLES
½ cup (65 g) diced carrot
½ cup (65 g) green peas
1 small red bell pepper, seeded and diced

3 tbsp (45 ml) neutral oil, divided
3 cloves garlic, minced
¾ tsp salt, or to taste
¼ tsp white pepper
Chopped scallions, for garnish

Note: Kala namak (black salt) adds a certain aroma similar to that of eggs, due to its sulfur content. It is used in a lot of vegan recipes to mimic the flavor of eggs. You can, of course, opt to use regular sea salt in recipes that call for kala namak.

Place the rice in a large bowl and break apart with a spoon to separate the grains. This is most easily done if the rice has been cooled prior to cooking. If using freshly cooked rice, leave the rice to cool in front of a fan for 10 minutes for the moisture to evaporate.

Prepare the tofu: Press the tofu for at least 10 minutes to drain any excess liquid (see page 11 for more details). Afterward, slice one-third of the tofu into ½-inch (1.3-cm) cubes. Place the remaining two-thirds of the tofu in a small bowl and mash with a fork or your hands. Set aside.

Heat a large skillet or wok over medium-high heat. Add 1 tablespoon (15 ml) of the oil. Once hot, add the tofu cubes and pan-fry them, flipping about every 2 minutes, until golden brown and crisp on all sides, about 10 minutes total. Meanwhile, in a small bowl, mix together the sugar and soy sauce. Add the mixture to the tofu cubes and let cook until the sugar caramelizes, about 2 minutes. Mix to coat the tofu well and then transfer the tofu to a small bowl. Set aside.

Prepare the vegetables: In the same pan over medium-high heat, add the carrot, green peas and bell pepper. Sauté together for 5 minutes. Remove from the pan and set aside with the tofu cubes.

Add another tablespoon (15 ml) of the oil. Over medium-high heat, add the mashed tofu. Season with turmeric and black salt. Mix well until the tofu turns yellow and resembles scrambled eggs. Move the tofu to the side of the pan.

Add the remaining tablespoon (15 ml) of oil. Sauté the garlic over medium-high heat for a minute, or until golden brown. Increase the heat and add the rice. Then, mix the tofu scramble into the rice. Add the tofu cubes and cooked vegetables. Season the fried rice with salt and white pepper, then mix everything together. Cook for 2 to 3 more minutes, then turn off the heat. Garnish with scallions, if desired. Enjoy your fried rice while it's still hot.

Unagi-Style Eggplant Rice Bowls

In this recipe, eggplants take the place of unagi, the Japanese word for freshwater eel, which is traditionally cooked the kabayaki way, whereby the fish is sliced in half, deboned, dipped in a sweet soy sauce–based sauce and cooked on a grill.

These unagi-style eggplants are cooked down in a rich savory and umami sauce until it absorbs all the delicious flavors! I enjoyed these over steamed short-grain rice and finished off with sesame seeds, scallions and Japanese seven-spice blend (togarashi) for a really satisfying and flavor-packed meal.

Makes 6 halves, 3 bowls
Prep Time: 10 minutes
Cook Time: 20 minutes

EGGPLANTS
3 medium-sized Chinese eggplants (about 1 lb [450 g])

UNAGI SAUCE
¼ cup (60 ml) soy sauce
2 tbsp (30 ml) mirin
2 tbsp (30 ml) sake or rice wine
¼ cup (55 g) packed cane sugar, or to taste
½ tsp grated fresh ginger

TO SERVE
3 cups (550 g) steamed short-grain rice
Sesame seeds
Japanese seven-spice blend (togarashi)
Chopped scallions

Prepare the eggplants: Using a fork, punch holes around each eggplant eight to ten times. Place the eggplants in a microwave-safe bowl. Sprinkle some water on the eggplants and cover them with a microwave-safe lid. Microwave on high for 4 minutes, or until the eggplants are tender, wrinkly and cooked through.

While the eggplants are cooking in the microwave, prepare the sauce: Heat a large saucepan over low heat and combine the sauce ingredients. Increase the heat to medium and simmer, stirring constantly, for 5 minutes, or until the sugar has dissolved. Once the sauce thickens slightly, lower the heat. Feel free to adjust the seasonings based on your desired taste.

Slice the cooked eggplants in half and remove the top stems. Carefully open up the eggplants. Place the eggplants, skin side down, in the saucepan. Baste with the sauce and cook over medium heat for 4 to 5 minutes, or until the eggplants absorb the sauce.

Turn off the heat and serve the eggplants over steamed short-grain rice. Garnish with sesame seeds, Japanese seven-spice blend and scallions. Enjoy while hot.

Japanese Yakisoba

One of the easiest noodle dishes you can whip up is yakisoba—Japanese stir-fried noodles—cooked with a savory and slightly tangy sauce. The vegetables you add are totally up to you, so this is a perfect way to use up leftover vegetables!

Serves 2

Prep Time: 10 minutes

Cook Time: 15 minutes

SAUCE

1½ tbsp (22 ml) soy sauce

2 tsp (10 ml) rice vinegar

2 tbsp (30 ml) tomato ketchup

2 tsp (10 g) cane sugar, or to taste

2 tbsp (30 ml) vegan oyster sauce (homemade recipe on page 156) or stir-fry sauce

⅛ tsp freshly ground black pepper

YAKISOBA

10 oz (285 g) cooked yakisoba or fresh ramen noodles

2 tbsp (30 ml) neutral oil

1 scallion, chopped, plus more for garnish (optional)

1 small white onion, sliced

1 small carrot, thinly sliced

8 cabbage leaves, chopped

1 small bell pepper, seeded and sliced

6 fresh shiitake mushrooms

Pinch of salt, or to taste

Japanese seven-spice blend (togarashi), for garnish

Prepare the sauce: In a small bowl, mix all the sauce ingredients together. Feel free to adjust the seasonings based on your desired taste. Set aside.

Prepare the yakisoba: If using cooked yakisoba noodles from packets, run them under warm water to separate or follow the package instructions. Carefully separate the noodles and drain away any excess water.

Heat a large skillet or wok over medium-high heat. Add the oil. Once hot, add the scallion and white onion. Sauté for 2 minutes, or until aromatic. Add the carrot, chopped cabbage, bell pepper, mushrooms and a pinch of salt. Increase the heat to high and cook the veggies until crisp with a bite on the outside but tender on the inside, 3 to 4 minutes. Add the prepared noodles and pour in the sauce. Mix everything together well and then cook for 2 to 3 more minutes, or until the noodles have absorbed the sauce. Taste the noodles and then add more seasoning, if needed.

Turn off the heat and then transfer the noodles to a bowl or plate. Garnish your yakisoba with more chopped scallion and Japanese seven-spice blend, if desired. Best enjoyed while hot.

Pad Thai

I absolutely love pad thai, and making this at home always leaves me reminiscing about trips to Thailand. I made my own vegan fish sauce (page 161) to use for this recipe and coat the noodles in a deliciously sweet and savory sauce. I made this dish with tofu for protein, added crunch from bean sprouts and peanuts, tang from lime and an extra kick of spice from chili powder!

Serves 3
Prep Time: 15 minutes
Cook Time: 25 minutes

SAUCE
¼ cup (55 g) coconut sugar or palm sugar

¼ cup (60 ml) vegan fish sauce (homemade recipe on page 161), plus more to taste (see notes)

1 to 2 tbsp (15 to 30 ml) soy sauce, plus more to taste if needed (see notes)

1 tbsp (15 ml) fresh lime juice

2 tbsp (32 g) tamarind puree (see notes)

NOODLES AND VEGETABLES
7 oz (200 g) block extra-firm tofu

8 oz (225 g) dried rice noodles, at least ⅛" (3 mm) thick

3 tbsp (45 ml) neutral oil

1 small red or white onion, sliced

2 cloves garlic, minced

2 cups (150 g) fresh bean sprouts, plus more for serving

1 scallion, sliced into 2" (5-cm) strips

TO SERVE
Fresh lime juice

½ to 1 tbsp (4 to 8 g) chili powder or red pepper flakes (optional)

Handful of sliced scallions or chives

2 tbsp (30 g) chopped roasted peanuts

Prepare the sauce: In a small bowl, combine all the sauce ingredients. Feel free to adjust the ingredient amounts according to your desired taste. Set aside.

Prepare the noodles and vegetables: Press the tofu for at least 10 minutes to drain any excess liquid (see page 11 for more details). Afterward, slice into ½-inch (1.3-cm) cubes.

Place the rice noodles in a large, heatproof bowl. Pour in enough boiling hot water to completely soak the noodles. Leave the noodles to soak for 6 to 7 minutes, or until they are white (no longer translucent), pliable and still very chewy. Drain the noodles and set aside.

Heat a large skillet or wok over medium-high heat. Add the oil. Once the oil is hot, add the tofu cubes. Pan-fry them, flipping about every 2 minutes, until golden brown and crisp on all sides, about 10 minutes total.

Move the tofu to the side of the pan and then add the onion and garlic. Sauté until cooked, about 1 minute. Add the rice noodles and then pour in the sauce.

Mix well, then cook for 4 to 5 minutes, or until the noodles are cooked through but still a little chewy. Lower the heat to medium, then mix in the bean sprouts and strips of scallion. Taste the noodles and feel free to add more soy sauce or vegan fish sauce, as desired. Cook for another 2 minutes, then turn off the heat once the bean sprouts are tender.

Serve the noodles in two bowls, each with a generous squeeze of lime juice, chili powder or red pepper flakes, scallions or chives, peanuts and bean sprouts, if desired. Mix and enjoy your pad thai while it's still hot.

Notes: If you're using store-bought vegan fish sauce, start with 1 tablespoon (15 ml) or use soy sauce, since store-bought vegan fish sauce can be much saltier! You can replace the tamarind puree with a mix of 2 tablespoons (30 ml) of fresh lime juice and 2 tablespoons (28 g) of coconut sugar or palm sugar.

Yuxiang Eggplant Noodles

These bowls of noodles are topped with eggplants cooked in a meaty, fragrant and spicy sauce! The thick and rich sauce coats the noodles really well, so mix everything together while it's still warm and serve immediately.

Serves 2
Prep Time: 15 minutes
Cook Time: 20 minutes

EGGPLANTS
3 medium-sized Chinese eggplants (about 12 oz [340 g])

1 tsp coarse salt, for soaking

SAUCE
1 tbsp (15 ml) soy sauce

1 tbsp (15 ml) Chinkiang (Chinese black) vinegar

1 tbsp (15 ml) Shaoxing wine or dry sherry

1 tbsp (8 g) cornstarch

2 tbsp (30 g) cane sugar, or to taste

½ cup (120 ml) room-temperature vegetable broth or water

NOODLES
¼ cup (25 g) dried textured vegetable protein (TVP; see note)

5 oz (140 g) dried wheat noodles of choice

2 tsp (10 ml) neutral oil

TO STIR-FRY
3 tbsp (45 ml) neutral oil

1 small onion, diced

3 cloves garlic, minced

1½ tsp (5 g) minced fresh ginger

1 small red bell pepper, seeded and diced

2 tbsp (32 g) chili broad bean paste (doubanjiang)

¼ to ½ tsp salt, or to taste

Chopped scallions, for garnish (optional)

Prepare the eggplants: Slice the eggplants into batons 3 inches (7.5 cm) long and 1 inch (2.5 cm) thick. Place them in a large bowl. Sprinkle them with the coarse salt, then pour in enough room temperature water to submerge the eggplants. Leave the eggplants to sit in the salted water for at least 10 minutes.

Prepare the sauce: In a small bowl, mix together all the sauce ingredients until the cornstarch has dissolved. Set aside.

Prepare the noodles: Place the TVP in a strainer set over a bowl. Pour boiling hot water over the TVP, enough to submerge it. Let it soak for at least 5 minutes, or until rehydrated.

Meanwhile, bring a medium-sized pot of water to a boil over high heat. Once boiling, add the noodles and cook until still very chewy, around 1 to 2 minutes less than the package instructions. Remove the noodles from the water and rinse with running water. Divide the noodles between two bowls and sprinkle each bowl with half of the oil, then mix. This is to prevent the noodles from sticking together. Set the bowls aside.

Stir-fry the vegetables: Heat a large skillet or wok over medium-high heat. Add the oil. Once hot, add the onion, garlic and ginger. Sauté for 1 to 2 minutes, or until aromatic. Add the bell pepper and bean paste. Increase the heat to high and cook for 2 minutes, or until the bell pepper is tender.

Drain the eggplants from their water. Add the sliced eggplants to the pan along with the bell pepper. Over medium-high heat, cook until tender, about 6 minutes. Meanwhile, stir the sauce again to ensure that the starch doesn't stick to the bottom of the bowl. Lower the heat to medium, then pour in the sauce mixture while stirring with a spatula. Season with the salt, adjusting the amount to your taste if desired. Increase the heat to medium-high and simmer until the sauce thickens, about 2 minutes. Turn off the heat and then immediately divide the sauce between the two noodle bowls. Mix the sauce and noodles together. Garnish with chopped scallions, if desired. Serve while hot and saucy.

Note: You can replace the TVP with ⅔ cup (45 g) of diced shiitake mushrooms.

Soy Sauce–Braised Noodles

Prepare your bowls and chopsticks! These noodles are super flavorful, earthy and cooked down in a rich soy-based sauce. They're perfect for sharing as a whole meal in itself with extra vegetables or even your protein of choice, but you can also enjoy them along with your favorite side of tofu and vegetables.

Serves 4
Prep Time: 15 minutes
Cook Time: 20 minutes

1 oz (30 g) dried shiitake mushrooms (7 or 8 pieces)

6.5 oz (180 g) dried wheat or lo mein noodles

3 tbsp (45 ml) neutral oil

1 medium onion, sliced

3 cloves garlic, minced

3 cups (215 g) chopped cabbage

1 tbsp (15 ml) Shaoxing wine or dry sherry

2 cups (480 ml) mushroom water (from soaking the shiitake mushrooms) or vegetable broth

1½ tbsp (22 ml) dark soy sauce

2 tbsp (30 ml) soy sauce, or to taste, divided

1 tbsp (15 g) dark brown sugar

⅛ tsp ground white pepper

1 tbsp (8 g) cornstarch

2 tbsp (30 ml) room-temperature water

Handful of fresh chives, chopped

Place the dried mushrooms in a bowl with 2 cups (480 ml) of boiling water and soak for 10 to 15 minutes, or until rehydrated. Remove the mushrooms from the water, reserving all the mushroom water. Slice the mushrooms into ½-inch (1.3-cm)-thick pieces.

Bring a medium-sized pot of water to a boil over high heat. Once boiling, lower the heat to medium-high, then add the noodles. Cook until still very chewy, 2 minutes less than the package instructions, then drain the noodles. It's best to undercook the noodles because they will continue to cook in the sauce later on.

Meanwhile, heat a large skillet or wok over medium-high heat. Add the oil. Once hot, sauté the onion and garlic for 1 minute. Add the rehydrated mushrooms and cabbage and leave untouched for 2 minutes, or until lightly browned, before mixing and leaving the remaining side to lightly brown as well. Increase the heat to high and add the wine. Mix well with the cabbage and mushrooms until the wine evaporates.

Pour in the mushroom water or vegetable broth, dark soy sauce, 1 tablespoon (15 ml) of the soy sauce, and the sugar and pepper. Mix the sauce well and bring to a boil over medium-high heat, 3 to 4 minutes. Once boiling, add the noodles and simmer for 2 minutes.

Meanwhile, in a small bowl mix together the cornstarch and water to make a slurry. Pour the cornstarch slurry into the noodles while continuously stirring. Once the sauce thickens and is absorbed by the noodles, turn off the heat. Taste the noodles and season with up to 1 tablespoon (15 ml) of the remaining soy sauce, if needed. Add the chopped chives and then mix well. Serve while hot.

Singaporean Flat Rice Noodle Stir-Fry
(Char Kway Teow)

This char kway teow is reminiscent of my trips to Singapore, where I enjoyed a plate of these noodles in its food courts (also called hawker centers) that are filled with all the best food. They're stir-fried flat rice noodles cooked with tofu, bean sprouts and onions in a rich, sweet and savory sauce with tofu "egg."

Makes 2 servings
Prep time: 10 minutes
Cook time: 20 minutes

4.5 oz (125 g) dried wide flat rice noodles, at least ⅜" (1 cm) wide

7 oz (200 g) extra-firm tofu, divided

SAUCE
1 tbsp (15 ml) soy sauce

1½ tsp (8 ml) vegan oyster sauce (homemade recipe on page 156) or stir-fry sauce

1½ tbsp (22 ml) sweet soy sauce (kecap manis; homemade recipe on page 161)

1 tsp chili sauce of choice

STIR-FRY
4 tbsp (60 ml) neutral oil, divided

1 tbsp (15 ml) sweet soy sauce (kecap manis)

¼ cup (40 g) sliced onion

3 cloves garlic, minced

½ tsp ground turmeric

⅛ tsp kala namak (black salt) or sea salt

2 cups (150 g) bean sprouts

1 oz (30 g) fresh chives, chopped into 2" (5-cm) pieces

Place the noodles in a large bowl and pour enough boiling hot water into the bowl to completely submerge the noodles. Move the noodles around, then leave them to sit for 8 to 10 minutes, or until white (no longer translucent), still very chewy and pliable. Drain the noodles and set them aside.

Meanwhile, press the tofu for at least 10 minutes to drain any excess liquid (see page 11 for more details). Afterward, divide the tofu into two equal portions. Slice one portion into ½-inch (1.3-cm)-wide strips. Mash the other portion in a small bowl. Set both aside.

Prepare the sauce: In a small bowl, mix together all the sauce ingredients, then set aside.

Once the tofu is ready, heat a large cast-iron skillet over high heat. Add 2 tablespoons (30 ml) of the oil. Once hot, add the tofu strips in a single layer. Cook for 3 to 4 minutes on each side, and then flip over to crisp on the remaining side. Add the kecap manis and mix well. Leave the tofu to cook until lightly charred, then move it to the side of the pan.

In the same pan over high heat, add the remaining 2 tablespoons (30 ml) of oil. Add the onion and garlic. Sauté until tender and slightly charred, about 1 minute. Add the chewy noodles and then pour in the sauce. Mix well, then cook the noodles for 2 to 3 minutes, or until they absorb the sauce and are cooked through.

Move the noodles to the side of the pan. Lower the heat to medium-high, then add the mashed tofu. Sprinkle with the turmeric and salt. Mix everything well until the tofu is evenly yellow from the turmeric and resembles scrambled eggs.

Add the bean sprouts and chives. Mix everything together. Increase the heat to high and cook the noodles for another 2 to 3 minutes, or until the bean sprouts and chives are cooked.

Turn off the heat and then transfer the noodles to a plate. Serve immediately while it's still hot.

Spicy Dan Dan Noodles

This bowl of noodles is a slightly simplified version of the Szechuan classic—but rest assured that it doesn't skimp on taste and flavor! You'll get the delicious numbing spice from the Szechuan pepper all while enjoying the meaty texture of minced tofu. The noodles are enveloped in a rich, fragrant sauce that'll leave you asking for more.

Serves 2
Prep Time: 10 minutes
Cook Time: 20 minutes

TOFU AND NOODLES

8 oz (225 g) extra-firm tofu

1 tbsp (15 ml) sesame oil

1 tbsp (15 ml) hoisin sauce

1½ tsp (8 ml) Shaoxing wine or dry sherry

Pinch of Chinese five-spice powder (optional)

1 tbsp (15 ml) soy sauce

5 oz (140 g) green leafy vegetables of choice (bok choy, spinach, etc.)

5 oz (140 g) dried thin white wheat noodles or other wheat noodles of choice

2 tsp (10 ml) neutral oil

SAUCE

1 to 2 tbsp (15 to 30 ml) soy sauce, or to taste

1 tbsp (16 g) Chinese sesame paste (see note)

1 tsp cane sugar

Pinch of Chinese five-spice powder (optional)

¼ tsp ground Szechuan pepper

2 tbsp (30 ml) chili-garlic oil with sediment (homemade recipe on page 157), or to taste

1 tbsp (15 ml) sesame oil

1 clove garlic, minced

2 tbsp (30 ml) hot broth from the noodles or vegetable broth

GARNISHES (OPTIONAL)

Chopped roasted peanuts

Chopped scallions

Prepare the tofu and noodles: Press the tofu for at least 10 minutes to drain any excess liquid (see page 11 for more details). Afterward, transfer the tofu to a bowl and then crumble with your hands or a fork.

Heat a large skillet or wok over medium-high heat. Add the sesame oil. Once hot, add the crumbled tofu. Add the hoisin sauce, wine, five-spice powder (if using) and soy sauce. Mix well and cook, stirring about every 2 minutes, until the tofu dries up and resembles minced meat, about 10 minutes total.

While the tofu cooks, bring a medium-sized pot of water over high heat. Once boiling, blanch your leafy vegetables for 3 to 4 minutes, or until they're cooked to your desired doneness. Then, remove the veggies from the water, rinse with cold water and set aside. Add the noodles to the pot and cook until chewy (al dente), according to the package instructions. Drain the noodles from the water, reserving the water to use for the sauce later. Then, divide between two bowls and add some oil to the noodles and mix to coat well. This is to prevent the noodles from sticking. Set the noodles aside.

While the noodles cook, prepare the sauce: in a large bowl, mix all the sauce ingredients together. Adjust the seasonings based on your desired taste. Divide between the two noodle bowls.

Top the noodles with the minced tofu, blanched greens and chopped peanuts and scallions, if desired. Mix everything together and serve. Feel free to add more hot broth from the pot to loosen the noodles, as needed.

Note: Not to be confused with tahini, Chinese sesame paste is made with roasted white sesame seeds, giving it that nice light-brown color with a more robust flavor. Meanwhile, tahini is made with raw white sesame seeds, which have a nuttier flavor. Look for it at Asian markets or online.

Tasty Tofu Dishes

This chapter is a reflection of my love for tofu. These humble blocks of curdled soy, also known as bean curd, are often set aside for their bland taste, but when prepared and cooked well, they can pack so much flavor and easily become the star of the dining table. Here you'll find everything from crumbled tofu cooked to resemble minced meat for Spicy Thai Basil Tofu (page 70), all the way to slabs of tofu cooked in a tasty and really umami sauce—to replicate the usual pork—for Char Siu Tofu (page 58).

Tofu isn't just a perfect protein-packed meat substitute, but also the perfect vessel to carry all the flavor in saucy dishes, as it acts as a sponge when pressed well to release its excess liquid. You'll want to give these recipes a go and test out on your tofu-skeptic friends and family to see how these can change their opinion on tofu altogether.

Char Siu Tofu

These are slices of tofu cooked down in a rich, sweet and savory sauce. This dish is delicious as is, but is best enjoyed with a bowl of steamed rice or with freshly cooked noodles. The slices are also delicious placed in steamed buns to make Char Siu Tofu Gua Baos (page 22). The sauce is deliciously savory with a perfect balance of sweetness and a hint of spice.

Serves 2
Prep Time: 10 minutes
Cook Time: 25 minutes

TOFU

1 lb (450 g) extra-firm tofu

3 tbsp (45 ml) neutral oil

SAUCE

2 tbsp (30 ml) hoisin sauce

5 to 6 tbsp (70 to 85 g) dark brown sugar, or to taste

1 tbsp (15 ml) soy sauce

1 tsp minced garlic

½ tsp grated fresh ginger

2 tbsp (30 ml) Shaoxing wine or dry sherry

½ tsp Chinese five-spice powder

2 tsp (10 ml) sriracha (adjust according to desired heat)

TO SERVE

Toasted sesame seeds (optional)

Chopped scallions (optional)

Blanched vegetables, steamed rice and/or buns

Prepare the tofu: Press the tofu for at least 10 minutes to drain any excess liquid (see page 11 for more details). Turn the block of tofu on its side and slice it through the middle to make 1-inch (2.5-cm)-thick slabs. You will have 2 to 3 slabs depending on the size and thickness of your tofu.

Prepare the sauce: In a small bowl, mix together all the sauce ingredients. Set aside.

Heat a large, nonstick skillet over medium-high heat. Add the oil. Once hot, add the tofu slabs. Pan-fry the tofu until lightly browned on each side, about 4 minutes per side. Remove the tofu from the pan and then let it cool for 5 minutes before slicing each slab into 1-inch (2.5-cm)-thick strips.

In the same pan, over medium heat, add the sauce and stir well until the sugar dissolves. Increase the heat to medium-high and bring the sauce to a boil. Once boiling, lower the heat to medium. Stir the sauce to prevent the sugar from sticking to the pan and burning. Taste the sauce and feel free to add more sugar, if desired. Afterward, add the sliced tofu to the pan, then scoop the sauce to pour over the top of the tofu pieces. Continue to cook and baste the tofu until it has absorbed some of the sauce, 7 to 8 minutes. Increase the heat to high; once the sauce thickens, about 2 minutes, turn off the heat.

Garnish your tofu with sesame seeds and scallions, if desired. Enjoy your Char Siu Tofu as is, with blanched veggies, with rice or as filling for buns to make gua baos (page 22).

Mapo Tofu

Mapo Tofu is one of my favorite tofu dishes. The use of silken tofu gives it a smooth and velvety texture that goes so well with the spicy, numbing sauce containing Szechuan pepper and fermented black beans. It's comfort in a bowl and perfect for a really hearty meal with some steamed rice.

Serves 3
Prep Time: 10 minutes
Cook Time: 20 minutes

½ cup (50 g) dried TVP (textured vegetable protein) (makes 1 cup [150 g] rehydrated; see note)

21 oz (600 g) silken tofu

2 tbsp (30 ml) neutral oil, for cooking

½ tsp ground Szechuan pepper, or 1 tsp whole crushed Szechuan peppercorns

½ cup (30 g) chopped scallions, plus more for garnish

2 cloves garlic, minced

1 cup (75 g) finely diced fresh shiitake mushrooms

1 tbsp (16 g) fermented black beans

1 tsp cane sugar

2 tsp (10 ml) chili-garlic oil with sediment (homemade recipe on page 157)

1 tsp gochujang (Korean chili paste) or sriracha (adjust according to desired heat)

1 tbsp (15 ml) soy sauce, or to taste

1½ cups (360 ml) vegetable broth

2 tbsp (16 g) cornstarch

¼ cup (60 ml) room-temperature water

Salt, to taste

Steamed rice, to serve

Place the TVP in a medium-sized heatproof bowl. Add boiling water to cover and let it soak for at least 5 minutes, or until doubled in size. Afterward, strain out the liquid and set the TVP aside.

Carefully slice the silken tofu into 1-inch (2.5-cm) pieces and set aside on a plate.

Heat a large skillet or wok over medium-high heat. Add the oil. Once hot, add the Szechuan pepper. Sauté for 2 minutes, or until aromatic. Add the scallions and garlic, and cook for 1 minute before adding the mushrooms. Cook the mushrooms and TVP for 2 to 3 minutes. Once cooked, add the black beans, sugar, chili-garlic oil, gochujang and soy sauce. Mix well. Carefully add the chopped silken tofu, and try not to break it up further. Increase the heat to medium-high, add the vegetable broth and simmer until it boils.

In a small bowl, mix together the cornstarch and room-temperature water until the starch has dissolved.

Once the tofu mixture is boiling, add the cornstarch slurry, carefully stirring as to not break apart the tofu. Cook for 2 to 3 more minutes, or until the sauce thickens. Season with salt or more soy sauce, as needed, to taste.

Turn off the heat and garnish with more scallions. Enjoy your tofu while hot with steamed rice.

Note: You can replace the TVP with 2 cups (150 g) of finely diced fresh shiitake mushrooms; do not add boiling water to the mushrooms.

Sweet and Spicy Crispy Korean Tofu
(Dubu Gangjeong)

In this dish, crispy pieces of pan-fried tofu are cooked in a sticky, spicy, sweet and slightly tangy sauce. "Dubu" means "tofu" in Korean, while gangjeong is a type of starchy Korean sweet treat that is fried to achieve a crisp coating. This is a savory tofu version and you can enjoy it with bowl of steamed rice or as is!

Serves 2
Prep Time: 10 minutes
Cook Time: 25 minutes

TOFU
14 oz (400 g) extra-firm tofu
½ tsp salt
2 tbsp (16 g) cornstarch

SAUCE
1 tbsp (16 g) gochujang (Korean chili paste)
½ cup (120 ml) room-temperature vegetable broth or water
2 tbsp (30 ml) pure maple syrup or other liquid sweetener, or adjust to taste
1 tbsp (15 ml) sesame oil
⅓ cup (80 ml) tomato ketchup
1 tbsp (15 ml) soy sauce
1 tsp rice vinegar
2 tsp minced garlic
1 tbsp (8 g) cornstarch

TO COOK AND SERVE
Neutral oil, for cooking
1 small white onion, sliced
2 cloves garlic, minced
1 small bell pepper, seeded and sliced
Steamed rice or cooked noodles, to serve
Toasted sesame seeds and chopped scallions, for topping (optional)

Prepare the tofu: Press the tofu for at least 10 minutes to drain any excess liquid (see page 11 for more details). Slice into 1-inch (2.5-cm) cubes. Place the tofu in a bowl. Sprinkle the salt and cornstarch onto the tofu cubes. Toss the tofu to coat well in the starch.

Prepare the sauce: In a small bowl, mix together all the sauce ingredients until well incorporated. Set aside.

Heat a large, nonstick or cast-iron skillet over medium-high heat. Add enough oil to the pan to cover the surface. Once the oil is hot, place the coated tofu cubes in the pan.

Pan-fry the tofu cubes, flipping about every 2 minutes until golden brown and crisp on all sides, about 10 minutes total. Afterward, remove the tofu from the oil and transfer to a paper towel–lined plate or a strainer to drain any excess oil.

In the same pan, over medium-high heat, sauté the onion and garlic until aromatic, about 2 minutes. Add the bell pepper and sauté until tender, about 2 minutes.

Add the sauce. Lower the heat to medium and simmer, continuing to stir, until the sauce has come to a boil. Add the crispy tofu and mix it into the sauce. Cook for 3 to 4 minutes, or until the sauce has thickened.

Turn off the heat. Enjoy the tofu with a bowl of steamed rice or cooked noodles. Feel free to garnish with toasted sesame seeds and chopped scallions, if desired.

Singaporean Chili Tofu

One of the most memorable dishes I've tried in a food court (a.k.a. hawker center) in Singapore was chili crab with its spicy yet thick and really luscious sauce. It's a delicate balance of sweet, spicy and salty, packed with a fragrant blend of garlic, shallots and ginger. Here, we have crispy-coated tofu, cooked in a similar sauce, that traditionally has beaten eggs mixed into it. For this vegan version, I opted to use silken tofu, which adds a nice texture to the richness of the sauce. You'll find yourself wanting more and more of this sauce, whether it's with rice, noodles or fried buns (mantou).

Serves 2
Prep Time: 20 minutes
Cook Time: 20 minutes

1 lb (450 g) extra-firm tofu

2½ tbsp (25 g) cornstarch

¼ tsp salt

5 to 6 bird's eye chiles (adjust according to desired heat)

2 small shallots, halved and peeled

8 cloves garlic, crushed and peeled

1 (1" [2.5-cm]) slice fresh ginger, peeled

TO COOK

¼ cup (60 ml) neutral oil

1 tbsp (16 g) fermented soybean paste (doenjang)

1¼ cups (300 ml) water or vegetable broth

2 tbsp (30 g) cane sugar, or to taste

4 tbsp (60 ml) tomato ketchup

2 oz (55 g) silken tofu, mashed (optional)

1 tbsp (8 g) cornstarch

2 to 3 tbsp (30 to 45 ml) room-temperature water

TO SERVE

Chopped cilantro (optional)

Steamed buns, cooked rice or noodles

Press the tofu for at least 10 minutes to drain any excess liquid (see page 11 for more details). Slice into 2-inch (5-cm) cubes. In a shallow bowl, mix together the cornstarch and salt. Place each cube in the cornstarch mixture and coat evenly.

Chop off the top stems of the chiles. Place the chiles, shallots, garlic and ginger in a food processor and pulse or process until minced. You can also opt to mince these aromatics using a knife. Set aside.

Heat a large nonstick skillet over medium-high heat. Add the oil. Once the oil is hot, add the coated tofu cubes. Pan-fry the tofu, flipping about every 2 minutes, or until golden brown and crisp on all sides, about 10 minutes total. Remove the tofu from the pan and transfer to a strainer or a paper towel–lined plate lined to drain any excess oil. Do not cover the tofu; this will help to prevent it from getting soggy.

To the same pan in the remaining oil, add the chile mixture. Sauté for 3 minutes over medium heat, or until aromatic and the shallots are slightly translucent. Add the soybean paste, water or vegetable broth, sugar and ketchup, then mix until the paste is diluted and the sugar is dissolved, about 3 minutes. Add the silken tofu (if using) and carefully mash it with your spatula before mixing well into the sauce. Increase the heat to medium-high and bring the sauce to a boil.

Meanwhile, in a small bowl, mix together the cornstarch and water. Once the sauce mixture is boiling, lower the heat to medium and then stir in the cornstarch slurry while mixing. Continue to stir until the sauce has thickened, about 2 minutes. Add the pan-fried tofu and then carefully mix to coat in the sauce well. Cook for 2 more minutes, then turn off the heat.

Garnish the tofu with chopped cilantro, if desired. Enjoy hot with steamed buns that you can dip into the sauce. You can also enjoy this with rice or noodles.

Japanese Tofu Tonkatsu

These are slabs of tofu dipped in a batter and coated in bread crumbs before being fried to a crisp. I then finished them off with a drizzle of homemade tonkatsu sauce for a deliciously tasty and crunchy bite. This is one of those really versatile tofu dishes that you can enjoy as is, with steamed rice or as a filling in between slices of bread for a tofu tonkatsu sandwich!

Serves 2
Prep Time: 20 minutes
Cook Time: 15 minutes

TOFU TONKATSU

1 lb (450 g) extra-firm tofu

1½ tsp (9 g) salt, divided

½ cup (65 g) all-purpose flour

1 tbsp + 2 tsp (13 g) cornstarch

1 tsp baking powder

½ cup (120 ml) room-temperature water

1 cup (60 g) Japanese or panko bread crumbs, plus more as needed

Neutral oil, for frying

TONKATSU SAUCE

⅓ cup (80 ml) tomato ketchup

1 tbsp (15 ml) soy sauce

1 tsp cider vinegar

1 tsp dark brown sugar or other sugar, or to taste

TO SERVE

Toasted sesame seeds

Shredded cabbage

Miso-Sesame Dressing (page 138), for the cabbage

Lemon wedges

Cooked rice (optional)

Prepare the tofu tonkatsu: Press the tofu for at least 10 minutes to drain any excess liquid (see page 11 for more details). Afterward, slice into 1-inch (2.5-cm)-thick slabs. You may be able to slice your tofu into two or three slabs, depending on the thickness of your tofu. Sprinkle ½ teaspoon of the salt over the tofu and rub onto both sides.

Prepare the batter in a medium-sized bowl by mixing together the flour, cornstarch, baking powder, remaining 1 teaspoon of salt and the water until smooth. Spread the bread crumbs on another plate or tray. Place a tofu slab in the batter, then coat with the bread crumbs. Repeat this step for the rest of the tofu.

Heat a large skillet over high heat. Add enough oil to submerge the tofu slabs at least halfway up the sides. Once the oil is hot and bubbling, carefully add two or three coated pieces of tofu, depending on the size of your pan. The tofu should immediately sizzle when placed in the oil. Be sure to have them spaced at least 1 inch (2.5 cm) apart from one another. Fry for 4 to 5 minutes, or until golden brown, flipping the tofu halfway through if it is not completely submerged in the oil. Once the tofu is golden brown, remove each piece from the oil and transfer to a strainer or a paper towel–lined plate to drain any excess oil. Let cool for 2 to 3 minutes, uncovered, to maintain the crispiness.

Meanwhile, make the tonkatsu sauce: In a small bowl, combine all the sauce ingredients. Mix everything together until the sugar has dissolved. Taste the sauce and feel free to adjust accordingly.

Slice the cooked tofu katsu diagonally into 1-inch (2.5-cm) pieces. Drizzle with the tonkatsu sauce and sprinkle with toasted sesame seeds. This is best enjoyed while hot and crispy with a side of shredded cabbage with miso-sesame dressing, a squeeze of lemon and rice, if desired.

Filipino Tofu Steak (Bistek Tagalog)

A childhood favorite of mine was Filipino bistek, which is basically beef steaks cooked in a savory and slightly sour sauce with sautéed onions. This, of course, is a vegan version using slabs of tofu and is still oh-so-satisfying that you'll find yourself scooping up that sauce to soak the tofu and your favorite grain.

Serves 3 to 4
Prep Time: 15 minutes
Marinate Time: 40 minutes
Cook Time: 15 minutes

TOFU
1½ lb (680 g) extra-firm tofu

MARINADE
5 tbsp (75 ml) soy sauce
¼ cup (60 ml) fresh lemon juice (from 1 lemon)
½ tsp freshly ground black pepper
1 tsp coconut sugar
½ tsp garlic powder

TO COOK
2 tbsp (30 ml) neutral oil, plus more as needed
2 small red onions, sliced into rings
2 cloves garlic, minced
½ cup (120 ml) vegetable broth
1 tsp coconut sugar, plus more to taste if needed
Salt, to taste

Steamed rice, to serve

Prepare the tofu: Press the tofu for at least 10 minutes to drain any excess liquid (see page 11 for more details).

Prepare the marinade: While the tofu is pressing, in a shallow bowl or plate, mix together the marinade ingredients.

Slice the tofu into ¾-inch (2-cm)-thick square pieces. Place each slice of tofu into the marinade. Let marinate for at least 40 minutes, flipping each tofu slice over halfway through marinating.

Cook the tofu: Heat a large skillet or nonstick skillet over medium heat. Add the oil. Sauté the onions until slightly translucent and tender, about 3 minutes. Remove the onions from the pan and set aside. Add more oil to the pan, if needed. Add the marinated tofu, reserving the leftover marinade, increase the heat to medium-high and pan-fry for 3 to 4 minutes, or until lightly browned. Flip the tofu over, then cook the other side until lightly browned as well. Remove the tofu from the pan and transfer to the plate of onions. Set aside.

Lower the heat to medium and add the garlic into the pan. Sauté for 2 minutes. Add the reserved marinade, increase the heat to medium-high and stir to deglaze the pan. Add the vegetable broth and sugar. Add the pan-fried tofu back to the pan and let simmer until the mixture boils. Add the sautéed onions and lower the heat to medium. Taste the sauce and then season with more sugar and salt, as needed, to taste. Turn off the heat and enjoy the tofu with steamed rice while hot.

Spicy Thai Basil Tofu (Pad Krapow)

This recipe is inspired by Thai basil chicken that I used to love eating at Thai restaurants. Instead of ground chicken, I used minced tofu to re-create that meaty texture and cooked it down in a really flavorful, spicy and savory sauce that I enjoyed with jasmine rice.

Serves 3
Prep Time: 10 minutes
Cook Time: 20 minutes

TOFU
1 lb (450 g) extra-firm tofu

SAUCE
2 tbsp (30 g) coconut sugar or palm sugar
¼ cup (60 ml) vegetable broth
4 to 5 tbsp (60 to 75 ml) vegan fish sauce (homemade recipe on page 161; see note)
1 tbsp (15 ml) soy sauce, or to taste (see note)
1 tsp cornstarch

TO COOK
3 tbsp (45 ml) neutral oil
1 small red onion, diced
3 cloves garlic, minced
2 green chiles, sliced, seeded if desired
2 bird's eye chiles, sliced, seeded if desired
1 small red bell pepper, seeded and diced
1 packed cup (50 g) fresh Thai basil leaves
Pinch of ground white pepper

TO SERVE
Sliced bird's eye chile (optional)
Steamed jasmine rice

Prepare the tofu: Press the tofu for at least 10 minutes to drain any excess liquid (see page 11 for more details). Afterward, place the tofu in a bowl and crumble it with your hands or a fork. Set aside.

Prepare the sauce: In a small bowl, mix together all the sauce ingredients. Feel free to adjust the measurements depending on your desired taste. Set aside.

Heat a large, nonstick skillet or wok over medium-high heat. Add the oil. Once hot, sauté the red onion until translucent, 1 to 2 minutes. Add the garlic, chiles and bell pepper. Lower the heat to medium and sauté for 3 to 4 minutes, or until the bell pepper is cooked through. Add the mashed tofu. Increase the heat to high and let the tofu lightly brown, stirring it about every 2 minutes, until it dries up and resembles minced meat, about 10 minutes total.

Stir the sauce again and then pour it into the tofu. Mix the tofu well, lower the heat to medium-high, then add the Thai basil. Mix well and cook for 2 minutes, until the basil leaves have wilted. Season with white pepper and more soy sauce, if needed. Turn off the heat and add more sliced chiles, if desired. Enjoy while hot with steamed rice.

Note: If using store-bought vegan fish sauce, start with the smaller amount and lessen the soy sauce, as needed, because store-bought fish sauce is much saltier than my homemade version on page 161.

Garlic, Tofu and Broccoli Stir-Fry

Here's a simple yet satisfying tofu stir-fry with broccoli! This is inspired by the broccoli dishes I love to get at our local Chinese restaurants that are often cooked with a lot of aromatic garlic, ginger and scallion. This dish is also packed with protein and a delicious way to get in some green veggies!

Serves 4
Prep Time: 15 minutes
Cook Time: 20 minutes

TOFU
14 oz (400 g) extra-firm tofu

STIR-FRY SAUCE
3 tbsp (45 ml) soy sauce, plus more to taste if needed

1 tbsp (15 g) cane sugar, or to taste

¼ cup (60 ml) vegetable broth

1½ tsp (4 g) cornstarch

TO COOK
Neutral oil, for frying

1 tsp grated ginger

6 cloves garlic, minced

1 scallion, chopped

4 cups (400 g) raw broccoli florets (from 1 head)

Pinch of salt

¼ cup (60 ml) vegetable broth or water

Steamed rice, to serve

Prepare the tofu: Press the tofu for at least 10 minutes to drain any excess liquid (see page 11 for more details). Afterward, slice into 1-inch (2.5-cm) thick squares.

Prepare the sauce: In a small bowl, mix together all the sauce ingredients. Set aside.

Heat a large skillet (choose one with a lid) over medium-high heat. Add enough oil to cover the surface of the pan. Once the oil is hot and bubbles, carefully add each piece of tofu. Pan-fry the tofu until golden brown, about 4 minutes on each side. Remove from the oil and transfer to a strainer or a paper towel–lined plate to drain any excess oil. Feel free to remove some of the oil in the pan, as this will be the same pan for stir-frying.

In the same pan over medium-high heat, sauté the ginger, garlic and scallion until aromatic, about 2 minutes. Add the broccoli florets. Add a pinch of salt and the vegetable broth or water. Cover the pan with its lid, lower the heat to medium and let the broccoli cook for 3 minutes, or until cooked to your desired doneness. Remove the lid and add the fried tofu back to the pan.

Give the sauce a good mix to make sure the starch doesn't stick to the bottom. Pour the sauce into the pan. Mix the tofu and broccoli well with the sauce. Over medium heat, cook for 3 to 4 more minutes, or until the sauce thickens. Taste the tofu and broccoli and add more soy sauce, to taste, if needed. Turn off the heat. Serve with steamed rice and enjoy while it's hot.

Fried Tofu with Black Bean and Chili-Garlic Oil

My grandma gave me a bottle of black bean garlic sauce that I've really been enjoying for stir-fries and sauces. They're fermented black beans and can be quite salty, but they add so much more depth to a dish and a little can go a long way!

These are crispy pieces of tofu cooked with the black bean garlic sauce and homemade chili-garlic oil. They are so fragrant and have that perfectly salty bite from the black beans.

Serves 2
Prep Time: 15 minutes
Cook Time: 20 minutes

1 lb (450 g) extra-firm tofu

Neutral oil, for frying

2 tbsp (30 ml) sesame oil

¼ cup (15 g) chopped scallion

1 dried chile, sliced (optional)

2 tsp (6 g) minced garlic

1 tbsp (15 g) fermented black beans or black bean garlic sauce

1 small red bell pepper, seeded and diced

1 tbsp (15 ml) chili-garlic oil (homemade recipe on page 157; adjust according to desired spiciness)

Press the tofu for at least 10 minutes to drain any excess liquid (see page 11 for more details). Slice into 1-inch (2.5-cm)-thick pieces.

Heat a large skillet over high heat. Add enough oil to completely submerge the pieces of tofu. Once the oil is hot and bubbling, carefully add the tofu. Fry for 5 to 6 minutes, or until the tofu pieces are golden brown and crisp.

Remove the tofu from the oil and transfer to a strainer or a paper towel–lined plate lined to drain any excess oil. Turn off the heat. Remove the oil from the pan.

To the same pan, over medium-high heat, add the sesame oil. Sauté the scallion, chile (if using) and garlic until aromatic, about 2 minutes. Add the black beans or black bean garlic sauce and bell pepper. Sauté for another 2 minutes. Add back the tofu and add the chili-garlic oil. Mix everything together and cook for another 2 minutes. Turn off the heat and serve while it's still hot and the tofu is crispy.

Soups, Stews and Braises for the Soul

As the chapter's title suggests, this section contains hearty food to warm your soul. Despite growing up in the Philippines where it's pretty much warm and humid all year long, I always found an excuse to cook up and enjoy a warm bowl of noodles. Try a bowl of Umami Tofu, Mushroom and Miso Ramen (page 81) that's inspired by those I've tried in the streets of Osaka in Japan. You can enjoy the best bowls by the street side in the middle of a cold night, slurping away until you've filled your belly with chewy ramen noodles and rich broth. For a lighter bowl of noodle soup, there's also Vietnamese Mushroom Pho (page 78), inspired by the bowls I had in Ho Chi Minh City (also known as Saigon), Vietnam, with the distinct aroma of all the spices and fresh herbs you can add upon being served the hot bowl of pho. In here, you'll also find hearty braises and stews that will keep you asking for more rice as you probably won't be able to prevent yourself from scooping up the sauce to enjoy with your grain.

Vietnamese Mushroom Pho (Pho Chay)

This phở chay ("chay" translates to "vegetarian" in Vietnamese) has a really aromatic and savory mushroom broth with a hint of sweetness. This recipe uses a mix of spices and is inspired by the bowls of phở I had in the streets of Ho Chi Minh City in Vietnam where locals have phở for breakfast from eateries that open very early in the morning. I like to enjoy my phở with a generous squeeze of lime juice and top it with more bean sprouts and fresh herbs, while also dipping the toppings in hoisin and chili sauce, which is how phở is commonly eaten in Southern Vietnam.

Serves 2
Prep Time: 20 minutes
Cook Time: 45 minutes

AROMATICS

1 large white onion, quartered

2 thumb-sized pieces fresh ginger, sliced ¼" (6 mm) thick

TOFU AND MUSHROOMS

7 oz (200 g) extra-firm tofu

1 tbsp (15 ml) vegan fish sauce (homemade recipe on page 161)

1 tsp cane sugar

¼ tsp Chinese five-spice powder

2 tbsp (30 ml) neutral oil

Pinch of salt

7 oz (200 g) fresh mushrooms of choice, sliced

NOODLES

7 oz (200 g) dried rice noodles, 3 to 5 mm thick

Boiling water, to soak noodles

Prepare the aromatics: Heat a small cast iron pan or skillet over high heat. Once smoking, add the onion and ginger. Cook until lightly charred, about 3 minutes on each side, then turn off the heat and transfer these to a bowl. Set aside.

Meanwhile, prepare the tofu and mushrooms: Press the tofu for at least 10 minutes to drain any excess liquid (see page 11 for more details). Slice into ¾-inch (2-cm)-thick pieces and place in a bowl. In a small bowl, mix together the vegan fish sauce, sugar and five-spice powder and then pour over the tofu to coat it with the sauce.

To the same pan used for the onion and ginger, add the oil and heat over medium-high heat. Once hot, add the tofu and add a pinch of salt. Pan-fry the tofu until crisp on both sides, about 6 minutes total. Remove the tofu from the pan and place on a plate. Add the mushrooms to the pan and cook until tender. Set the tofu and mushrooms aside for topping later on.

Prepare the noodles: Heat a large pot with water over high heat. Once the water boils, add in the rice noodles. Cook the noodles 1 to 2 minutes less than the package instructions or until chewy. Drain the noodles from the water. Afterward, run the noodles through cold water to stop the cooking and remove the starch. Set the noodles aside. Pour out the water from the pot.

(continued)

Vietnamese Mushroom Pho (Pho Chay) (continued)

BROTH
1½ tbsp (22 ml) neutral oil

1 fragrant or Korean pear, any variety, seeded and sliced into wedges

1 large carrot, peeled and cubed

1 cinnamon stick

5 dried star anise

3 whole cloves

8 cups (2 L) vegetable or imitation beef broth

4 pieces dried shiitake mushroom

½ to 1 tsp salt, or to taste

1 tsp cane sugar

2 tbsp (30 ml) vegan fish sauce (homemade recipe on page 161), plus more to taste

GARNISHES
½ cup (35 g) fresh bean sprouts

Fresh Thai basil leaves

Fresh cilantro leaves

Chopped scallion

Sliced red chiles (optional)

Fresh lime juice

FOR DIPPING
Hoisin sauce

Sriracha

Prepare the broth: In the same pot used to cook the noodles, add the oil, pear, carrot, cinnamon stick, star anise and cloves. Increase the heat to medium-high and sauté for 4 minutes until aromatic. Add the broth, dried shiitake mushrooms, charred onion and ginger. Cover the pot and simmer until the soup comes to a boil.

Once the soup boils, lower the heat to medium. Season the broth with the salt, sugar and vegan fish sauce. Feel free to adjust the seasoning based on your desired taste. Leave to simmer for another 15 minutes or even longer and allow the pear to cook down until very soft. Also, the longer the broth simmers, the stronger the flavors will be. Afterward, remove or strain the spices and aromatics from the broth. You can slice up the shiitake mushrooms and add to your bowls as toppings.

Before serving, you can quickly blanch the cooked rice noodles in the soup to warm them. To assemble, place the noodles, tofu and mushrooms in two bowls. Pour the hot soup into both bowls. Top them with bean sprouts, your herbs of choice and sliced red chiles, if desired. Finish with a squeeze of lime juice. You can dip the tofu and mushrooms in a mix of hoisin sauce and sriracha, if desired.

Umami Tofu, Mushroom and Miso Ramen

These are noodles in a rich miso broth topped with minced tofu, bok choy, mushrooms, corn, sesame seeds and a generous drizzle of rayu (Japanese chili oil). This takes me back to delicious bowls of ramen enjoyed in the small alleys of Osaka in Japan. You'll want bowlfuls of this umami and silky broth. Enjoy your hot bowl of noodles on a cold night and slurp away!

Serves 2
Prep Time: 15 minutes
Cook Time: 45 minutes

MINCED TOFU AND MUSHROOMS

7 oz (200 g) extra-firm tofu

2 tbsp (30 ml) sesame oil, divided

1 tsp minced garlic

1 tsp minced fresh ginger

1½ tbsp (22 ml) soy sauce

1½ tsp (8 ml) chili sauce or sriracha

1 tsp dark soy sauce (optional, for color)

4 oz (115 g) fresh mushrooms of choice, such as shiitake, shimeji or oyster

NOODLES AND TOPPINGS

2 servings dried instant or fresh ramen noodles

4 oz (115 g) bok choy or other leafy vegetables (spinach, mustard greens, etc.)

Prepare the tofu and mushrooms: Press the tofu for at least 10 minutes to drain any excess liquid (see page 11 for more details). Afterward, crumble the tofu in a small bowl with a fork until the pieces are mostly the size of minced meat.

Heat a medium-sized nonstick pan over medium heat. Add 1 tablespoon (15 ml) of the sesame oil. Once hot, sauté the garlic and ginger for 2 minutes, or until the garlic is slightly browned. Add the crumbled tofu. Season with soy sauce and chili sauce. Mix the tofu well, increase the heat to medium-high and cook, allowing the tofu to crisp undisturbed on one side for 3 to 4 minutes, before moving it around. Cook the tofu for 5 to 6 more minutes, moving it around every 2 minutes, to evenly brown on all sides. The tofu will slowly start to resemble cooked meat as the water evaporates. Add the dark soy sauce (if using). Mix well and then cook for another 3 to 4 minutes, or until golden brown throughout. Set the cooked tofu aside in a small bowl.

To the same pan, over medium-high heat, add the remaining 1 tablespoon (15 ml) sesame oil. Sauté the mushrooms for 2 to 3 minutes, or until cooked through. Set the mushrooms aside in a separate small bowl.

Prepare the noodles and toppings: Bring a large pot of water to a boil over high heat, then lower the heat to medium. Add the instant ramen noodles or other noodles of choice. Cook the noodles until still very chewy (al dente). You'll want very chewy noodles here since they'll continue to cook in the soup later on. Remove the noodles from the water (do not discard the hot water) and run them under cold water. Drain well and then divide the noodles between your two ramen bowls.

In the same pot and water used for the noodles, blanch the bok choy or other vegetables over medium-high heat for 3 to 4 minutes, or until slightly translucent and cooked to your liking. Turn off the heat and drain the vegetables, discarding the water from the pot. Set aside and then divide the vegetables between the ramen bowls of noodles.

(continued)

Umami Tofu, Mushroom and Miso Ramen (continued)

MISO BROTH

1 tbsp (15 ml) sesame oil or Japanese chili oil (rayu), divided

½ cup (25 g) sliced scallions, white and green parts separated

½ tsp Szechuan peppercorns (optional but highly recommended)

1 tbsp (16 g) Chinese sesame paste (see note)

2 tbsp (45 g) miso paste

2 cloves garlic, minced

3 cups (720 ml) vegetable broth

1 cup (240 ml) unsweetened soy or oat milk

1 tbsp (15 ml) soy sauce

¼ to ½ tsp salt, or to taste

TO ASSEMBLE

2 tbsp (20 g) corn kernels

Chopped scallions, for topping

Sesame seeds, for topping (optional)

Japanese chili oil (rayu) or sesame oil, for topping

Prepare the miso broth: Heat the same large pot used to cook the noodles to medium-high heat. Add half of the sesame oil or rayu. Once hot, add the chopped white parts of the scallion and Szechuan peppercorns (if using). Sauté for 2 to 3 minutes, or until the scallion is cooked through. Lower the heat to medium. Add the sesame paste, miso paste and garlic. Mix until well combined. While stirring, add the vegetable broth and soy milk. Keep stirring until the paste is diluted. Add the soy sauce and salt to taste. Cover the pot, increase the heat to high and bring the soup to a boil, 5 to 6 minutes. Once boiling, lower the heat to medium, then add the chopped green scallion. Taste the soup and feel free to adjust the seasonings based on desired taste. Add the remaining sesame oil or rayu. Mix well and then turn off the heat. Cover the pot to prevent the soup from cooling too fast.

Assemble and serve: To each ramen bowl of noodles and blanched vegetables, add half of the minced tofu, mushrooms and corn kernels. Pour half of the soup into each bowl. Top with the chopped scallion and sesame seeds. Finish off with a generous drizzle of rayu or sesame oil. Enjoy immediately while still hot.

Note: Chinese sesame paste is not the same as tahini. Chinese sesame paste is made with roasted white sesame seeds, giving it that nice light-brown color with a more robust flavor. Meanwhile, tahini is made with raw white sesame seeds, which have a nuttier flavor. Look for it at Asian markets or online. If needed, you can replace the Chinese sesame paste with 1 tablespoon (16 g) of plain peanut butter, 1½ teaspoons (5 g) of crushed toasted sesame seeds and 1 teaspoon of sesame oil.

Korean Kimchi Stew (Kimchi Jjigae)

Kimchi jjigae has a special place in my heart, mainly because I love kimchi and how much depth and flavor it can give to a dish. You'll only need one pot, or a Korean Ttukbaegi (earthenware bowl) or dolsot (stone bowl), for this recipe. Simply sauté a few of the ingredients before adding everything else and bringing to a boil. From there, you'll have a really tasty and comforting meal. Enjoying this with a bowl of steamed short-grain rice takes me back to those freezing winters in Seoul.

Serves 4
Prep Time: 10 minutes
Cook Time: 20 minutes

TOFU
7 oz (200 g) firm or extra-firm tofu

SOUP PASTE
1½ tbsp (12 g) gochugaru (Korean chili powder; adjust according to desired spiciness)

2 tbsp (30 ml) soy sauce

2 tsp (10 g) gochujang (Korean chili paste)

½ tsp minced garlic

Pinch of freshly ground black pepper

1 tbsp (15 ml) hon mirin or mirin

SOUP BASE AND TOPPINGS
1 tbsp (15 ml) sesame oil

1 medium-sized white onion, sliced

3 scallions, thinly sliced, plus more for topping

1 cup (160 g) vegan kimchi, preferably aged (homemade recipe on page 158)

4 medium-sized fresh shiitake mushrooms, sliced

7 oz (200 g) enoki mushrooms, separated

3 cups (720 ml) vegetable stock or water

Salt (optional)

TO SERVE
Steamed short-grain rice

Extra kimchi (optional)

Prepare the tofu: Press the tofu for at least 10 minutes to drain any excess liquid (see page 11 for more details). Slice into 1-inch (2.5-cm)-thick slices.

Prepare the soup paste: In a small bowl, mix together the soup paste ingredients until you have a well-combined paste. Set aside.

Prepare the soup base: Heat a medium-sized pot or a Korean clay pot over medium heat. Once hot, add the sesame oil. Add the onion and scallions, then sauté for 2 to 3 minutes, or until the onion is translucent and they are cooked through. Add the kimchi and soup paste, then sauté for 2 minutes. Add the mushrooms and tofu. You can arrange these around the pot, if you'd like. Pour in the vegetable stock. Cover the pot and bring the soup to a boil over medium-high heat, 5 to 6 minutes.

Once the soup boils, lower the heat to a simmer. Taste the soup and season with salt, as needed. If you're happy with the flavors, turn off the heat and garnish with more scallions, if desired. Enjoy the stew while it's hot with steamed short-grain rice and more kimchi on the side, if you'd like.

Japanese Buckwheat Noodle and Seaweed Soup
(Wakame Soba)

Try these chewy noodles in a light yet really warm and satisfying kombu broth topped with rehydrated wakame, mushrooms, chopped scallion and togarashi. This is one of my go-to dishes during trips to Japan and can be made with soba or udon noodles. There's really nothing like enjoying a hot bowl of noodles in the cold weather!

Serves 2
Prep Time: 15 minutes
Cook Time: 15 minutes

SOUP

2 (5" x 5" [12 x 12–cm]) pieces dried kombu

4 pieces dried shiitake mushroom

7 oz (200 g) dried buckwheat or soba noodles

6 cups (1.4 L) vegetable broth or mushroom and kombu broth from soaking

2 tbsp (30 ml) sake or rice wine

¼ cup (60 ml) hon mirin or mirin

¼ cup (60 ml) soy sauce

½ tsp salt, or to taste

TOPPINGS

2 tbsp (1 g) dried wakame

Boiling water, to rehydrate wakame

Rehydrated shiitake mushrooms, from the broth

Sprinkle of Japanese seven-spice blend (togarashi)

Chopped scallions

Prepare the soup: Presoak the kombu and dried shiitake overnight by placing these in a medium-sized bowl and covering with room-temperature water. If you're unable to soak them overnight, soak them for at least 10 minutes in boiling water. Make sure to cover them after pouring in the hot water to retain the steam. Do not discard the broth from the soaking process.

Bring a medium-sized pot of water to a boil over medium-high heat. Once boiling, add the dried noodles. Cook for 1 to 2 minutes less than the cooking time listed on the package instructions, or until the noodles are still very chewy and have a bite. Quickly drain the noodles from the water and run under cold water to remove any excess starch. Set the noodles aside by dividing between two bowls. Discard the water from the pot.

To the same pot, add the kombu and shiitake mushrooms along with the broth. Cover and bring the broth to a boil over medium-high heat. Once boiling, add the sake, mirin, soy sauce and salt to taste. Cook for another 6 to 7 minutes.

Prepare the toppings: While the soup cooks, rehydrate the dried wakame by placing it in a small bowl. Pour boiling water over the wakame and let it rehydrate for 2 to 3 minutes, or until quadrupled in size. Drain the water.

Remove the kombu and mushrooms from the broth. You can opt to slice the kombu and mushrooms to enjoy with the noodles.

Assemble the bowls by placing the wakame over the noodles along with the shiitake mushrooms and kombu. Pour the hot broth over the noodles and top with the seven-spice blend and chopped scallions. Enjoy immediately while hot and the noodles are still chewy.

Braised Tofu and Mushrooms in Ginger-Scallion Sauce

For this recipe, I cook tofu and mushrooms in a rich aromatic ginger and scallion sauce until each piece absorbs the flavor. This is one of those Chinese dishes that we'd often cook at home in a clay pot and serve right after cooking. The sauce is really flavorful and goes well with other vegetable dishes, such as Chinese Green Beans with Minced "Pork" (page 110) and Stuffed Chinese Eggplants (page 114), that are best enjoyed with your loved ones.

Serves 4
Prep Time: 15 minutes
Cook Time: 30 minutes

TOFU AND MUSHROOMS

21 oz (600 g) extra-firm tofu

6 shiitake mushrooms, fresh or dried and rehydrated

¼ cup (32 g) cornstarch

¾ tsp salt

Neutral oil, for frying

SAUCE

1 tbsp (15 ml) sesame oil

10 thin slices fresh ginger (about 0.3 oz [10 g] total)

4 cloves garlic, peeled and crushed

2 scallions, sliced into 2" (5-cm)-long strips

1 tbsp (15 ml) Shaoxing wine

2 cups (480 ml) vegetable broth or mushroom water (if using dried)

3 tbsp (45 ml) soy sauce, or to taste

1 tbsp (15 g) cane sugar

¼ tsp ground white pepper

1½ tsp (4 g) cornstarch

1 tbsp (15 ml) room-temperature water

Steamed rice, for serving

Prepare the tofu and mushrooms: Press the tofu for at least 10 minutes to drain any excess liquid (see page 11 for more details). Afterward, slice into 2-inch (5-cm) cubes.

Slice the mushrooms into ½-inch (1.3-cm)-thick pieces. Discard the tough stems, if necessary. Set the mushrooms aside for the sauce.

In a shallow bowl or plate, mix together the cornstarch and salt. Place each cube of tofu into the mixture to coat evenly.

Heat a large, nonstick skillet over medium-high heat. Add enough oil to the pan to cover the surface. Once the oil is very hot and has small bubbles, add the cornstarch-coated tofu. Pan-fry the tofu cubes, flipping around every 2 minutes until golden brown and crisp on all sides, about 10 minutes total. Remove the tofu from the pan and transfer to a strainer or a paper towel–lined plate to drain any excess oil.

Prepare the sauce: While the tofu is pan-frying, heat a large clay or regular pot over medium heat. Add the sesame oil. Sauté the ginger, garlic and scallions until aromatic, about 3 minutes. Add the mushrooms. Increase the heat to medium-high and then add the wine. Cook until the liquid evaporates, about 1 minute. Add the broth, soy sauce, sugar and pepper. Add the pan-fried tofu. Lower the heat to medium and simmer until the sauce comes to a boil, about 4 minutes.

In a small bowl, mix together the cornstarch and water. While mixing, pour the cornstarch slurry into the tofu mixture. Continue to simmer over medium heat, stirring occasionally, until the sauce thickens, about 3 minutes. Leave the tofu to cook for 2 to 3 more minutes to absorb the flavors. The sauce will continue to thicken from the cornstarch coating from the tofu as well. Serve this hot with a bowl of steamed rice.

Filipino Tofu Braised in Tomato Sauce (Afritada)

Afritada is a Filipino dish that's usually composed of meat, such as chicken or pork, cooked down in a rich tomato sauce with potatoes, carrots, bell peppers and sometimes even peas and sausage. With the Philippines having been a Spanish colony for over three centuries, Filipino cuisine has a lot of Spanish-derived dishes and this is one of them. I grew up eating a variety of tomato-based dishes, such as this braise, and love it served over rice. This version is just as good and flavorful with tofu cooked down in a really hearty tomato-based sauce, which I'd scoop up spoonfuls of to soak my rice in!

Serves 4
Prep Time: 20 minutes
Cook Time: 30 minutes

1 lb (450 g) extra-firm tofu

1 tbsp (15 ml) fresh lemon juice

3 tbsp (45 ml) soy sauce, divided

1 small red or white onion

2 small bell peppers (red and green), seeded

1 medium-sized carrot, peeled

1 large potato, peeled

2 tbsp (30 ml) neutral oil

2 cloves garlic, minced

2 to 3 cups (480 to 720 ml) vegetable broth (adjust as needed to thin sauce)

2 tbsp (32 g) tomato paste

2 tbsp (30 g) coconut sugar or other sugar, or to taste

Salt and freshly ground black pepper

¼ cup (30 g) fresh or frozen green peas (optional)

Steamed rice or your favorite cooked grain, for serving

Press the tofu for at least 10 minutes to drain any excess liquid (see page 11 for more details). Slice into 1-inch (2.5-cm)-thick cubes or rectangles. In a large bowl, mix together the lemon juice and 1 tablespoon (15 ml) of the soy sauce. Add the tofu and let marinate for at least 10 minutes.

Slice the onion, bell peppers, carrot and potato into 1-inch (2.5-cm) pieces, similar to the tofu.

Heat a large, nonstick skillet (choose one with a lid) over medium-high heat. Once hot, add the oil. Place the pieces of tofu in the pan and pan-fry until browned and crisp on one side, about 2 minutes. Flip the tofu over and then leave them to crisp on the remaining sides, about 10 minutes total. Remove the tofu and set aside on a plate.

Add the onion and garlic to the pan. Sauté over medium-high heat for 1 minute before adding the bell peppers. Sauté for 2 minutes before adding 2 cups (480 ml) of vegetable broth to start, along with the remaining 2 tablespoons (30 ml) of the soy sauce, the tomato paste and sugar. Add the carrot.

Cover the pan, then bring to a boil over high heat. Remove the lid and cook the carrot for 4 to 5 minutes, then add the potato. Cook for about 5 more minutes, until both are half-cooked, then add the pan-fried tofu. Lower the heat to medium-high and continue to simmer, mixing every 2 to 3 minutes to prevent the sauce from sticking to the pan. Taste the sauce and season with salt and pepper to taste.

Once the potato and carrot are cooked through, add the green peas (if using), and then thin down the sauce with ½ to 1 cup (120 to 240 ml) more broth as needed before bringing everything to another boil.

Feel free to add more salt and pepper or sugar as needed, depending on your desired taste. Turn off the heat and enjoy this afritada served with your favorite grain.

Thai Green Curry

A fragrant, spicy and creamy curry packed with tofu and vegetables! This is one of those recipes wherein you can opt to add whatever veggies you like, but eggplant, in my opinion, is essential in Thai curries. It's also important to fry the curry paste before mixing in the coconut milk to really release its aroma and get the best flavor!

Serves 3
Prep Time: 10 minutes
Cook Time: 20 minutes

TOFU AND CURRY

7 oz (200 g) extra-firm tofu

1 tbsp (15 ml) neutral oil, for sautéing

2 cloves garlic, minced

2 tsp (5 g) grated fresh ginger

3 to 4 tbsp (64 to 80 g) green curry paste (adjust according to desired heat)

1 (13.5-oz [400-ml]) can full-fat coconut milk

½ cup (120 ml) vegetable broth, plus more to thin as desired

1 tsp soy sauce or vegan fish sauce (homemade recipe on page 161)

1½ tbsp (23 g) coconut sugar, or to taste

1 medium-sized Chinese eggplant, sliced into 1½" (4-cm) pieces

7 oz (200 g) fresh or canned baby corn, halved lengthwise

1 small red bell pepper, seeded and sliced into strips

15 Thai basil or holy basil leaves

TO SERVE

Steamed jasmine rice

Fresh cilantro, for garnish (optional)

Fresh lime juice (optional)

Prepare the tofu and curry: Press the tofu for at least 10 minutes to drain any excess liquid (see page 11 for more details). Slice into 1-inch (2.5-cm) cubes. Set aside.

Heat a large pot over medium-high heat. Add the oil. Once hot, sauté the garlic and ginger for 2 minutes. Add the curry paste and sauté for another 2 to 3 minutes, stirring constantly, until very aromatic. Add the coconut milk and vegetable broth. Mix well to dissolve the paste. Season the curry with soy sauce or fish sauce and sugar. Lower the heat to medium and simmer for about 4 minutes, or until it's gently bubbling.

Once it's bubbling, add the tofu, eggplant, baby corn and bell pepper. Stir, then cover the pot and cook for another 5 minutes, or until the vegetables are tender.

Taste the curry and adjust the seasoning based on your desired saltiness and sweetness. Add additional vegetable broth to thin out the curry, if desired. Turn off the heat and mix in the basil leaves. Serve hot with steamed rice. Garnish with cilantro and a squeeze of lime, if desired.

Braised "Pork" (Lu Rou Fan)

This is one of those classic dishes that I grew up enjoying. It takes me back to meals sitting in humble, streetside open-air eateries in Taipei with a warm bowl of lu rou fan. This vegan version doesn't skimp on flavor: It's minced tofu cooked in an aromatic blend of spices and seasonings. I enjoy this over steamed rice with a side of preserved mustard greens; needless to say, it's comfort in a bowl.

Serves 3
Prep Time: 15 minutes
Cook Time: 30 minutes

BRAISED "PORK" TOFU

14 oz (400 g) extra-firm tofu

2 tbsp (30 ml) neutral oil

2 tbsp (30 g) dark brown sugar, or to taste

1 small shallot, finely diced

3 cloves garlic, minced

8 oz (225 g) fresh shiitake mushrooms, finely diced

3 tbsp (45 ml) soy sauce

⅛ to ¼ tsp Szechuan pepper powder (optional, for added heat)

2 tbsp (30 ml) Shaoxing wine or dry sherry

1 tsp Chinese five-spice powder

¼ tsp ground white pepper

1 tsp dark soy sauce (optional, for color)

1½ cups (360 ml) vegetable broth

1 tbsp (8 g) cornstarch

2 tbsp (30 ml) room-temperature water

TO SERVE

Steamed rice

Chopped scallions

Preserved mustard greens (sui mi ya cai) or blanched bok choy

Prepare the "pork" tofu: Press the tofu for at least 10 minutes to drain any excess liquid (see page 11 for more details). Place the tofu in a bowl. Crumble the tofu with your hands or a fork until it resembles ground meat. Set aside.

Heat a large skillet or wok over medium-high heat. Add the oil and let it heat for 2 to 3 minutes. Then, lower the heat to medium and add the brown sugar. Mix well until the sugar dissolves and caramelizes, about 3 minutes.

Add the shallot and garlic. Sauté in the sugar mixture for 2 minutes, or until translucent and lightly browned. Add the diced mushrooms and cook down for 2 minutes over medium-high heat.

Increase the heat to high, then add the crumbled tofu. Season with the soy sauce, Szechuan pepper, wine, five-spice powder, pepper and dark soy sauce (if using). Mix well until the alcohol evaporates. Lower the heat to medium-high again. Continue to cook the tofu, turning it every 2 to 3 minutes to evenly crisp the sides. The tofu will start to resemble minced pork as it cooks down and water from the tofu evaporates, about 8 minutes total. Once the tofu resembles minced meat, pour in the vegetable broth and simmer for about 2 minutes, or until the tofu absorbs some of the liquid.

In a small bowl, mix together the cornstarch and water. Pour the cornstarch slurry into the tofu mixture, continuously stirring, until the sauce thickens, about 1 minute. Lower the heat to medium, then simmer for another 2 minutes. Season the tofu more, if needed.

Turn off the heat and serve the braised "pork" tofu with steamed rice. Garnish with chopped scallions, and enjoy with a side of pickled mustard greens, if desired.

Asian-Inspired Twists

This chapter is a fusion of the West and Asia. Put together the distinct, pungent flavor and delicious crispiness of kimchi with salty cheese between a wheat tortilla, and you've got yourself a game-changing combo in the form of Kimchi Quesadillas (page 105). I don't know when I first tried this combo, but the acidity of the kimchi balances the heartiness of the cheese so well. You'll also find here an umami Charlie Chan Pasta (page 101)—think of a plate of saucy spaghetti coated in a luscious, really savory and umami sauce with a delicious crunch from roasted cashews. The recipes in this chapter are a reflection of my love for combining different cuisines and creating new experiences altogether that I hope you and your palate will enjoy.

Savory Scallion and Toasted Sesame Waffles

These waffles are inspired by my love for scallion pancakes, which I love to have for breakfast or as a snack whenever I visit Taipei. Waffles are a different twist, and are simpler to make. They're crisp on the outside and chewy on the inside, which I then drizzle with a generous amount of maple syrup. If you don't have a waffle maker, you can make a pancake version with a few adjustments. From each bite of this, you'll get a taste of scallions and toasted sesame!

Makes four or five 5" (12-cm) square waffles
Prep Time: 15 minutes
Cook Time: 15 minutes

DRY INGREDIENTS

1⅓ cups (175 g) all-purpose flour

1 tbsp (10 g) baking powder

¼ tsp Chinese five-spice powder

½ tsp sea salt

Pinch of ground white pepper (optional)

WET INGREDIENTS

⅓ cup (80 ml) neutral oil

1½ tbsp (22 ml) room-temperature water

¾ cup (180 ml) room-temperature unsweetened soy or oat milk

½ tsp toasted sesame oil

1 cup (50 g) chopped scallions, green parts only

2 tbsp (20 g) toasted sesame seeds

TO COOK AND SERVE

Neutral oil, for cooking

Pure maple syrup, for drizzling

Chopped scallions, for garnish

Preheat your waffle maker according to the manufacturer's instructions.

In a large bowl, mix together the dry ingredients.

In a medium-sized bowl, mix together the wet ingredients until well combined.

Stir the dry ingredients and pour in the wet mixture as you go. Mix until you no longer see any dry flour. A few lumps are okay. Add the chopped scallions and toasted sesame seeds. Mix everything until well combined. This will be a very thick batter.

Brush or spray a thin layer of oil onto your heated waffle maker. Scoop ⅓ cup (80 ml) of the batter (note that the amount of batter will depend on the size of your waffle maker) and pour it into the center of the waffle maker. Press the waffle maker closed and cook until the waffles are crisp on the outside and slightly browned on the edges. Repeat for the rest of the batter.

Serve the waffles with a generous drizzle of maple syrup and more chopped scallions, if desired. Enjoy the savory and sweet flavors!

Pancake Version

If you'd like to make pancakes instead of waffles, just replace the wet ingredients with the following measurements: 1 cup (240 ml) of room-temperature soy milk, ½ cup (120 ml) of room-temperature water, 1 tablespoon (15 ml) of neutral oil and ½ teaspoon of sesame oil.

This will yield a much thinner batter compared to the one for the waffles. To cook, simply heat a small or medium-sized nonstick pan over medium heat. Once hot, scoop ¼ cup (60 ml) of the batter into the pan and cook for 3 to 4 minutes, or until you start to see bubbles and the sides of the pancake start to dry up. Flip the pancake and cook for another 2 to 3 minutes. Repeat this step for the rest of the batter to make about ten 4-inch (10-cm) pancakes.

Charlie Chan Pasta

This is a vegan take on the famous Charlie Chan Pasta from a local pizza chain in the Philippines called Yellow Cab. After the first time I tried it years back, I kept coming back for more and more. Imagine a savory pasta but better: It's deliciously umami with a kick of spice from the sauce, earthiness from the mushrooms and crunch from the cashews.

Serves 3
Prep Time: 10 minutes
Cook Time: 20 minutes

SAUCE
3 tbsp (45 ml) soy sauce

2½ tbsp (38 ml) hoisin sauce

¾ cup (180 ml) water

1 tbsp (15 ml) Shaoxing wine or dry sherry

2½ tbsp (38 g) cane sugar, or to taste

2 tbsp (30 ml) sesame oil

1½ tsp (1 g) red pepper flakes

¼ tsp salt

1 tbsp (8 g) cornstarch

2 tbsp (30 ml) room-temperature water

PASTA
½ lb (220 g) dried spaghetti or other pasta of choice

2 tbsp (30 ml) toasted sesame oil

3 cloves garlic, minced

1 small onion, diced

¼ cup (15 g) chopped scallion, plus more for garnish

7 oz (200 g) fresh shimeji mushrooms or other mushrooms of choice

¼ cup (35 g) roasted cashews

Prepare the sauce: In a small bowl, mix together the soy sauce, hoisin sauce, water, wine, sugar, sesame oil, red pepper flakes and salt. Feel free to adjust the seasoning depending on your desired taste. Set aside. In another small bowl, mix together the cornstarch and water until you have a slurry. Set this aside as well.

Prepare the pasta: Bring a medium-sized pot of water to a boil over high heat. Once boiling, add the pasta. Cook the pasta according to the package instructions until it's al dente and still very chewy, as it will continue to cook with the sauce. Drain the pasta.

While the pasta is cooking, heat a large, nonstick pan or skillet over medium-high heat. Add the oil. Once hot, sauté the garlic, onion and scallion for 1 minute. Once aromatic, add the mushrooms and cook until tender, about 3 minutes. Pour in the sauce and bring to a boil over medium heat.

Once the sauce boils, give the cornstarch slurry a good stir and then add it to the sauce, stirring continuously until the sauce starts to thicken.

Add the cooked pasta and leave it to simmer for 2 to 3 minutes over high heat until it has absorbed some of the sauce. Stir the pasta well and then add the roasted cashews. Top with more sliced scallions, if desired. Enjoy while hot.

Miso Mushroom Burgers

These miso mushroom burgers are really earthy. The miso really gives an extra added layer of umami to the protein-packed patties that's really hearty and satisfying. You can enjoy the patties in the form of a burger or enjoy them with gravy and a side of mashed potatoes, too!

Makes 4 patties
Prep Time: 15 minutes
Cook Time: 30 minutes

MISO MUSHROOM PATTIES

1 tbsp (15 ml) neutral oil

1 small onion, diced

4 cloves garlic, minced

1 lb (450 g) fresh shiitake, portobello or baby bella mushrooms, sliced

1 tbsp (15 ml) soy sauce

¼ to ½ tsp salt, plus more to taste

1½ cups (280 g) cooked brown or black rice

3 tbsp (70 g) white miso paste

⅛ tsp freshly ground black pepper

⅔ cup (40 g) Japanese or panko bread crumbs

¼ cup (35 g) all-purpose flour, plus more if needed

1 tsp toasted sesame seeds

Neutral oil, for pan-frying

SRIRACHA MAYO

3 tbsp (45 ml) vegan mayonnaise

1 tbsp (15 ml) sriracha (adjust according to desired spiciness)

1 tsp toasted sesame seeds

TO SERVE AS BURGERS

Lettuce

Sliced tomatoes

Sliced onion

4 burger buns

Prepare the patties: Heat a large, nonstick skillet over medium-high heat. Add the oil. Once hot, sauté the onion and garlic for 2 minutes, or until aromatic. Add the sliced mushrooms. Increase the heat to high. Add the soy sauce and salt to taste. Cook the mushrooms for 3 minutes, or until tender. Turn off the heat and let the mushrooms cool for 5 minutes.

Transfer the mushrooms to a food processor along with the cooked rice, miso paste and pepper. Process or pulse the mushrooms until they are minced and well incorporated with the rice. Do not over-process; leave some chunks of mushroom. Transfer the mixture to a large bowl and then add the bread crumbs, flour and sesame seeds. Mix everything well with a spatula until the mixture is well incorporated. Taste the mixture and add more salt, if needed.

Shape the mixture into a patty by scooping about ¾ cup (150 g) of the mixture. If the mixture doesn't hold together very well, feel free to add 1 to 2 tablespoons (8 to 15 g) more flour. Shape it into a ball and then carefully flatten with your palm until you have a 1-inch (2.5-cm)-thick patty. Repeat for the rest of the mixture. Feel free to shape the patties as you'd like.

Heat the same large, nonstick skillet over medium-high heat. Add enough oil to coat the surface of the pan. Once the oil is hot and bubbles, carefully place the patties in the pan. Cook on the first side until golden brown and crisp, about 5 minutes. Flip over the patties and cook the remaining side until browned and crisp, 5 more minutes. Turn off the heat and then remove the patties from the pan.

Prepare the sriracha mayo: In a small bowl, simply mix all the sriracha mayo ingredients together. Feel free to adjust the amount of sriracha based on your desired spiciness.

Assemble the burgers by placing some lettuce, tomatoes, onion and sriracha mayo, along with the patty, inside each bun. Feel free to get creative with your fillings!

Kimchi Quesadillas

I can't get over this game-changing combo: kimchi and cheese. Kimchi has that somewhat crisp, tangy taste that perfectly complements rich, salty cheese. I spread some gochujang on the tortilla wraps for extra heat and flavor and also added minced garlic and toasted sesame seeds. These are pan-fried to a crisp, oh so satisfying and perfect for snacking!

Makes 8 pieces
Prep Time: 10 minutes
Cook Time: 15 minutes

2 (8" [20-cm]) tortilla wraps

1 tbsp (16 g) gochujang (Korean chili paste)

1 tsp toasted sesame seeds

2 garlic cloves, minced

1 cup (120 g) shredded vegan mozzarella or Cheddar cheese

1 cup (160 g) vegan kimchi (homemade recipe on page 158)

1 tbsp (15 ml) neutral oil, for pan-frying

Lay out the tortilla wraps on a plate or flat surface. Spread half of the gochujang on half of each wrap. Sprinkle with toasted sesame seeds and minced garlic. Add half of the cheese shreds on half of each wrap. Add half of the kimchi on top of the cheese and fold the wraps in half.

Heat a large, nonstick pan over medium heat. Add the oil. Carefully place the two folded tortilla wraps in the pan and press down with a spatula. Cook for 4 to 5 minutes, or until golden brown and crisp. Flip the quesadillas over and repeat for the other side. Turn off the heat and transfer the quesadillas to a plate.

Slice each half into quarters, to make a total of 8 pieces. Serve while still hot!

Note: You can also opt to add other fillings, such as black beans and sliced jalapeños, to the quesadillas along with the cheese and kimchi!

Sweet and Spicy Cauliflower Bites

I love snacking on these crisp pieces of battered and coated cauliflower in a sweet and spicy sauce! You can opt to fry or bake the cauliflower pieces, too. This is one of my favorite ways to enjoy cauliflower and it is also a family favorite at home.

Serves 3
Prep Time: 30 minutes
Cook Time: 25 minutes

SAUCE

1 to 2 tbsp (16 to 32 g) gochujang (Korean chili paste) or other chili sauce of choice (adjust according to desired spiciness)

½ cup (120 ml) room-temperature vegetable broth or water

2 tbsp (30 ml) pure maple syrup or other liquid sweetener, or to taste

⅓ cup (80 ml) tomato ketchup

1 tbsp (15 ml) soy sauce

1 tsp cider vinegar

2 tsp (6 g) minced garlic

1 tbsp (15 ml) sesame oil

1 tbsp (8 g) cornstarch

CAULIFLOWER

⅓ cup (45 g) all-purpose flour

1 tbsp (8 g) cornstarch

1 tsp baking powder

1 tsp salt

½ cup (120 ml) room-temperature water

1 to 1½ cups (55 to 85 g) Japanese or panko bread crumbs, plus more as needed

1 lb (450 g) cauliflower florets (from 1 large head)

Neutral oil, for cooking

Sesame seeds, for garnish

Chopped scallion, for garnish

Prepare the sauce: In a medium-sized bowl, mix together all the sauce ingredients Adjust the chili paste and other ingredients depending on your preference. Set aside.

Prepare the cauliflower: In a large bowl, mix together the flour, cornstarch, baking powder, salt and water until you have a smooth batter. Place the bread crumbs in a medium-sized bowl or plate.

Dip one cauliflower floret in the batter to coat well. Transfer to the bread crumbs and press the crumbs to the cauliflower until it is breaded throughout. Set aside on another plate once coated. Repeat this for the rest of the florets until all the pieces are coated.

Heat a large skillet over high heat with enough oil to submerge the cauliflower at least halfway. Once the oil is hot and sizzles when some bread crumbs are added, add the coated cauliflower florets and cook until golden brown, moving them to brown each side every 2 minutes or so, about 5 minutes total. Once golden brown, set the cauliflower aside in a strainer or a paper towel–lined plate to drain any excess oil.

Alternatively, to bake, preheat your oven to 350°F (180°C) and line a baking sheet with parchment paper or a silicone mat. Place the coated cauliflower on the prepared pan and brush each piece with some oil. Bake for 35 to 40 minutes, or until crisp, flipping halfway through the baking time.

Optionally, now cook the cauliflower in the sauce: If you fried the cauliflower, remove the oil from the pan and set the pan over medium heat. If you opted to bake the cauliflower, heat a medium-sized saucepan over medium heat. Add the sauce to the pan and then simmer over medium heat, mixing constantly until it thickens, 3 to 4 minutes. Once the sauce thickens, lower the heat and add the cauliflower. Mix to coat in the sauce. Alternatively, without adding the cauliflower, you can cook down the sauce until it thickens, transfer it to a bowl and use as a dip for the cauliflower or mix in the browned cauliflower right before serving to keep the pieces crispy.

Garnish the cauliflower with sesame seeds and chopped scallion, if desired. Enjoy immediately while hot.

Simply Satisfying Vegetables and Sides

I think we can all agree that vegetables deserve more recognition, especially at the dining table. Not only do they pack so many nutrients, but they also come in so many different shapes and sizes that, when prepared well, they can really become a main in itself. I put together recipes for this chapter with hopes that you'll discover new ways to cook and prepare your vegetables and enjoy them even more!

Green beans, when dry-fried on a sizzling hot wok, can become beautifully blistered and pack that unique smoky flavor and delicious crunch. They become even more delicious when cooked with minced tofu or "pork," as I've done for the classic Chinese Green Beans with Minced "Pork" dish (page 110) that my whole family loves. There are also mushrooms, humble little fungi that have a somewhat meaty texture and are packed with earthy, umami flavors, which become a perfect main ingredient for Korean Bulgogi Mushrooms (page 118), to be enjoyed with your favorite side dishes (banchan) and of course rice. And let's not forget the other humble vegetables, such as eggplant, bell pepper and potato, that when cooked in a delicious sauce and served together can easily become a favorite.

Chinese Green Beans with Minced "Pork"

Here we have fresh green beans that are pan-fried until lightly blistered, then tossed with minced tofu "pork" that's been cooked in a fragrant blend of ginger, chili-garlic oil and toasted sesame seeds. This easy stir-fry is one of the dishes I grew up enjoying, and it's packed full of flavor! Don't be surprised if, like me, you find yourself reaching for seconds, and even thirds.

Serves 2 to 3
Prep Time: 10 minutes
Cook Time: 30 minutes

TOFU
14 oz (400 g) extra-firm tofu

GREEN BEANS
12.5 oz (350 g) fresh green beans
2 tbsp (30 ml) neutral oil
¼ tsp salt

MINCED "PORK"
1 tbsp (15 ml) neutral oil
1 small onion, diced
½ tsp minced ginger
1½ tsp (4 g) minced garlic
1½ tsp (8 ml) chili-garlic oil, with sediment (homemade recipe on page 157 or store-bought)
1 tbsp (10 g) toasted sesame seeds
1½ tbsp (22 ml) hoisin sauce
1 tsp dark brown sugar
1 tbsp (15 ml) soy sauce, or to taste
1 tsp dark soy sauce
1 tbsp (15 ml) Shaoxing wine or dry sherry (optional but highly recommended)

Whole or sliced bird's eye chile, for garnish (optional)

Prepare the tofu: Press the tofu for at least 10 minutes to drain any excess liquid (see page 11 for more details). Place the tofu in a bowl. Crumble the tofu with your hands or a fork until it resembles ground meat. Set aside.

Prepare the green beans: Snap both ends off each green bean with your hands and then break it in half to remove the strings or veins.

Heat a large skillet or cast-iron pan over medium-high heat. Once hot, add the oil.

Increase the heat to high, then add the green beans. Leave untouched for 2 to 3 minutes, or until browned on one side. Move the beans around and repeat this step until the beans are blistered and slightly wrinkly, about 10 minutes total. Sprinkle the salt onto the beans and mix well. Remove the beans from the pan and set aside.

Prepare the "pork": In the same pan used for the beans, add the oil and lower the heat to medium. Sauté the onion and ginger until aromatic and the onion is translucent, about 1 minute. Add the minced garlic and cook for another minute, or until the garlic is lightly browned.

Add the crumbled tofu to the pan. Season with the chili-garlic oil, toasted sesame seeds, hoisin sauce, brown sugar, soy sauce and dark soy sauce. Mix well. Increase the heat to high and add the wine (if using). Mix well as the alcohol evaporates, then lower the heat to medium-high again to continue to cook the tofu. Leave the tofu to cook, turning it every 2 to 3 minutes to evenly crisp the sides. The tofu will start to resemble minced pork as it cooks down and the water from the tofu evaporates.

Once the tofu resembles minced pork, add back the green beans and cook for another 3 to 4 minutes. Turn off the heat, then add the whole or sliced chile for extra heat, if desired. Enjoy while hot.

Japanese Stir-Fried Vegetables (Yasai Itame)

This is a really easy Japanese vegetable stir-fry that you'll commonly find in most Japanese restaurants. It is one of those quick dishes you can pull together with whatever veggies you have on hand, but an essential element is the cabbage, which gives a crunch and sweetness to the dish. It's essential to stir-fry the ingredients over high heat to make sure the vegetables are crunchy on the outside for that nice bite when you enjoy them!

Serves 2
Prep Time: 10 minutes
Cook Time: 10 minutes

1 oz (28 g) dried wood ear mushrooms (makes 1 cup [90 g] rehydrated)

2 tbsp (30 ml) neutral oil, for cooking

½ large white onion, sliced

1 small green bell pepper, seeded and sliced

½ large carrot, peeled and julienned

8 oz (225 g) cabbage, chopped

3 fresh shiitake mushrooms, sliced

2 tbsp (30 ml) soy sauce

¼ tsp salt, or to taste

Pinch of freshly ground black pepper, or to taste

3 tbsp (45 ml) vegetable broth or water

1 tsp rice vinegar (optional)

1 scallion, sliced into 2" (5-cm) lengths

Rehydrate the wood ear mushrooms by placing them in a large bowl and leaving to soak in hot water for 7 to 8 minutes or in room-temperature water overnight. Once rehydrated, slice the mushrooms into 1-inch (2.5-cm) pieces. Set aside.

Heat a large skillet or wok over high heat. Add the oil. Once hot, sauté the onion and bell pepper for 2 minutes, or until tender. Add the carrot, cabbage, shiitake and wood ear mushrooms, plus the soy sauce and salt. Sprinkle with the black pepper. Mix well and then add the vegetable broth or water and the rice vinegar (if using). Cook down the vegetables until tender. Do not overcook, as you'll want them to still be crunchy on the outside. Mix in the scallion.

Taste the vegetables and season with more salt and black pepper to taste, if needed. Turn off the heat and serve while hot.

Stuffed Chinese Eggplants

If you're looking for a new way to cook up your eggplant apart from the usual baked or stir-fried methods, then you need to try stuffing them! I love the velvety texture of eggplants and really enjoy them with a hearty and flavorful tofu filling. These eggplants are delicious with rice or noodles, and the filling is also delicious as is!

Makes 8 eggplants
Prep Time: 15 minutes
Cook Time: 30 minutes

TOFU AND EGGPLANTS
9 oz (250 g) extra-firm tofu
2 lb (900 g) Chinese eggplants (8 eggplants)

SAUCE
1 cup (240 ml) vegetable stock
1 tbsp (15 ml) hoisin sauce
1½ tbsp (12 g) cornstarch
1 tsp sriracha or other chili sauce
1 tbsp (15 g) dark brown sugar
2 cloves garlic, minced
1 tbsp (15 ml) sesame oil
1 tbsp (15 ml) Shaoxing wine or dry sherry
2 tbsp (30 ml) soy sauce

FILLING
2 tbsp (30 ml) neutral oil
1 small white onion, finely diced
1 tsp minced fresh ginger
¼ tsp ground Szechuan pepper (optional)
½ small carrot, peeled and finely diced
1 small red bell pepper, seeded and finely diced
3 oz (85 g) fresh shiitake or other mushrooms, finely diced
2 scallions, sliced, plus more for garnish
Sliced chiles, for garnish (optional)

Prepare the tofu and eggplants: Press the tofu for at least 10 minutes to drain any excess liquid (see page 11 for more details). Place the tofu in a bowl. Crumble the tofu with your hands or a fork then set aside.

While the tofu is being pressed, puncture each eggplant four or five times around its body, using a fork. Place the eggplants in a microwave-safe dish and cover with a microwave-safe lid. Microwave for 2 minutes on high, or until the eggplants are wrinkly on the outside and tender to the touch. Flip the eggplants over and microwave, covered, for another 2 minutes on high. Let cool for 5 minutes. Alternatively, you can boil your eggplants in a pot of water until tender, about 6 minutes.

Prepare the sauce: In a medium-sized bowl, mix together all the sauce ingredients and adjust to your taste, then set side.

Prepare the filling: Heat a large skillet or wok over medium-high heat. Add the oil. Sauté the onion, ginger and Szechuan pepper (if using) until aromatic, about 2 minutes. Add the crumbled tofu, carrot, bell pepper, mushrooms and scallions. Sauté until the bell pepper and mushrooms are cooked through and the tofu is slightly golden brown, about 4 minutes. Continue to cook, turning to lightly crisp it, for another 2 minutes. The tofu will start to resemble minced meat as the water from the tofu evaporates.

Give the sauce a good mix again. Lower the heat to medium and pour the sauce into the pan. Stir well until the sauce thickens, 2 minutes. Taste the tofu and adjust the seasoning as needed. Turn off the heat and set the pan aside.

Slice through the middle of each eggplant lengthwise and carefully open them. Scoop a generous amount of the filling into each eggplant. Garnish with chopped scallion and sliced chile, if desired. Enjoy with rice or as is.

Eggplant, Potato and Bell Pepper Stir-Fry
(Di San Xian)

Di san xian (地三鲜) literally translates from Chinese to "three treasures of the earth" and is a dish made up of eggplant, potato and bell pepper. It is really popular in northern China, and for good reason, since the ingredients have an amazing blend of textures— you get a velvety bite from the eggplant, crispy potatoes and really fresh bell pepper.

Serves 2
Prep Time: 15 minutes
Cook Time: 20 minutes

SAUCE
1 tbsp (15 ml) Shaoxing wine or dry sherry
2 tbsp (30 ml) soy sauce
½ tsp cane sugar, or to taste
1 tsp toasted sesame oil
¼ cup (60 ml) vegetable broth
1½ tsp (4 g) cornstarch

STIR-FRY
2 medium-sized Chinese eggplants (about 9 oz [250 g] total)
1½ tsp (9 g) salt, plus more to taste
2 tbsp (16 g) cornstarch
10 oz (300 g) russet or Yukon Gold potato, peeled
1 small red bell pepper
1 small green bell pepper
3 tbsp (45 ml) neutral oil
2 scallions, thinly sliced
3 cloves garlic, minced
Steamed rice, for serving

Prepare the sauce: In a small bowl, mix together all the sauce ingredients. Set aside.

Prepare the stir-fry: Slice the eggplants horizontally in half, then into 1-inch (2.5-cm)-thick angled pieces. Place the eggplants in a large bowl. Add the salt and toss to coat the eggplants. Soak them in room-temperature water for 10 minutes. Then, drain the water and dry them with paper towels. Place the cornstarch in a large bowl, then add the eggplants. Toss them with your hands or a spoon to coat well in the cornstarch.

Meanwhile, while the eggplants are soaking, slice the potato and both bell peppers into 1-inch (2.5-cm) cubes and pieces, respectively. Set aside.

Heat a large skillet or wok over medium-high heat. Add the oil. When hot, add the potatoes. Cook for 3 to 4 minutes until lightly browned on one side. Flip the potato over and then leave the other side to lightly brown as well, another 3 to 4 minutes. Once the potato is cooked through, remove from the oil and set aside.

To the same pan, add the cornstarch-coated eggplants. Cook over medium-high heat for 4 to 5 minutes, moving it around every minute to evenly crisp on all sides. Once crisp and cooked through, remove from the pan.

To the same pan, add the scallions and garlic and lower the heat to medium. Sauté for 2 to 3 minutes, or until tender. Increase the heat to high and add the bell peppers. Cook for 2 minutes, or until tender.

Lower the heat to medium. Give the sauce a good stir again. While mixing with a spatula, add the sauce mixture to the pan. Continue to stir until the sauce has thickened, about 2 minutes. Add the sautéed potatoes and eggplants and mix into the sauce. Increase the heat to medium-high and cook for another 2 minutes, or until the sauce has been absorbed by the veggies and is thick. Season the vegetables with salt to taste. Serve and enjoy warm with rice.

Korean Bulgogi Mushrooms

If there's one thing I love about mushrooms, it's how meaty their texture can be and how well they absorb sauces! These king oyster mushrooms are packed full of flavor from the bulgogi sauce that's a perfect balance of sweet and savory. You can enjoy this wrapped in fresh lettuce or with steamed rice and Korean side dishes (banchan).

Serves 3 to 4
Prep Time: 15 minutes
Cook Time: 20 minutes

MUSHROOMS
1 lb (450 g) king oyster or trumpet mushrooms

BULGOGI SAUCE
¼ cup (60 ml) soy sauce

2 tbsp (28 g) packed dark brown sugar

1½ tsp (4 g) grated fresh ginger

1 tsp gochujang (Korean chili paste)

2 tbsp (30 ml) toasted sesame oil

3 cloves garlic, minced

⅓ cup (85 g) finely grated Asian pear or pear puree

1 tsp toasted sesame seeds

Pinch of freshly ground black pepper

TO COOK AND SERVE
1 tbsp (15 ml) neutral oil

1 small onion, thinly sliced

Fresh lettuce

Steamed rice

Vegan kimchi (homemade recipe on page 158)

Chopped scallions, for garnish (optional)

Sesame seeds, for garnish (optional)

Prepare the mushrooms: Slice the king oyster mushrooms in half horizontally. Cut them into 3- to 4-inch (7.5- to 10-cm)-long and 1-inch (2.5-cm)-thick strips. Alternatively, you can just shred or break them apart with your hands.

Prepare the sauce: In a large bowl, mix together the sauce ingredients until the sugar is diluted. Feel free to adjust the seasonings depending on your preference. Add the mushroom strips. Mix together to evenly coat the mushrooms.

Cook the mushrooms: Heat a large cast-iron skillet or wok over medium-high heat. Add the oil. Once hot, add the onion. Sauté for 2 to 3 minutes, or until the onion is translucent and lightly browned. Add the mushrooms, including the sauce that has not been absorbed. Moving the mushrooms every 2 to 3 minutes, cook for 7 to 8 minutes, or until they have absorbed the sauce and are lightly browned.

Turn off the heat and serve hot with fresh lettuce, steamed rice and kimchi, if desired. Top with chopped scallion and sesame seeds, if you'd like.

Mixed Mushroom Foil Bake

These mushrooms are wrapped in a foil basket and cooked down in a delicious umami miso sauce. This is one of those recipes that requires only a few minutes of your time and minimal cleanup! You'll need to prep the mushrooms and the sauce, then for the rest of the time, you just let the oven do its thing. This is inspired by the foil yakis I'd enjoy in local Japanese restaurants. You can also keep leftovers by just simply wrapping them back up in the foil and reheating in the oven again before serving.

Serves 2
Prep Time: 10 minutes
Cook Time: 35 minutes

BAKING SAUCE

1½ tbsp (22 ml) hon mirin or mirin

1 tbsp (15 ml) soy sauce, plus more to taste if needed

1½ tsp (10 g) white miso paste

TO BAKE

1 tbsp (15 ml) melted vegan butter or neutral oil

1 medium-sized white onion, thinly sliced

10 oz (300 g) fresh mixed mushrooms of choice (I used shiitake, king oyster and oyster; see note)

2 tsp (6 g) minced garlic

TO SERVE

Chopped scallion

Lemon wedges

Cooked short-grain rice (optional)

Preheat your oven to 350°F (180°C). Prepare a sheet of aluminum foil to measure 12 x 18 inches (30 x 45 cm). Then, set out a medium-sized baking sheet or baking dish, large enough to fit the piece of aluminum foil into.

Prepare the baking sauce: In a small bowl, mix together the baking sauce ingredients until well incorporated. Feel free to adjust the measurements according to your preference.

Place the aluminum foil on the baking sheet or in the baking dish. Add the vegan butter and place the onion, mushrooms and garlic in the center of the foil. Carefully scrunch the sides of the foil together and upward until you form a pouch with an opening only at the top. Seal all the other sides of the pouch well to prevent the sauce from seeping out. Then, pour the sauce into the mushrooms. Seal the pouch completely, then bake it for 30 to 35 minutes, or until the mushrooms are cooked through.

Carefully open the pouch, garnish with the chopped scallion, squeeze some lemon juice on top and pour in soy sauce, as desired, to taste. Enjoy while hot as is, or with a bowl of steamed short-grain rice.

Note: For the mushrooms, you can also opt to use enoki, baby bella, button and shimeji mushrooms!

Kung Pao Mushrooms

You'll love these bite-sized pieces of meaty mushrooms cooked in a sauce that's perfectly sweet, salty, tangy and spicy. The sauce is also really versatile—you can opt to adjust it based on your desired flavors. It's a really satisfying take on the Szechuan classic that's also become a Chinese takeout favorite across the globe.

Serves 3 to 4
Prep Time: 10 minutes
Cook Time: 20 minutes

MUSHROOMS

1 lb (450 g) fresh mushrooms (I used a mix of shiitake and king oyster mushrooms)

SAUCE

2 tbsp (30 ml) soy sauce

1 scallion, finely chopped

2 tsp (10 g) cane or dark brown sugar

1 tbsp (15 ml) Chinkiang (Chinese black) vinegar or rice vinegar

¼ cup (60 ml) vegetable broth

1½ tsp (4 g) cornstarch

½ to 1 tsp chili-garlic oil (homemade recipe on page 157)

TO COOK AND SERVE

3 tbsp (45 ml) neutral oil, divided

1 tsp minced fresh ginger

4 cloves garlic, minced

1 small red onion, diced

2 dried chiles or 1 bird's eye chile, sliced

1 tsp ground Szechuan pepper, or 1½ tsp (4 g) whole Szechuan peppercorn (optional)

¾ cup (100 g) seeded and diced red bell pepper

½ cup (75 g) roasted peanuts

Salt, to taste

Chopped scallion, for topping

Steamed rice, to serve

Prepare the mushrooms: Slice the mushrooms into ¾-inch (2-cm)-thick pieces. Set aside.

Prepare the sauce: In a small bowl, mix together all the sauce ingredients. Taste and feel free to adjust the measurements depending on your desired flavors. Set aside.

Cook the mushrooms: Heat a large skillet or wok over medium-high heat. Add half of the neutral oil. Once hot, add the diced mushrooms. Cook undisturbed for 2 minutes before moving them around in the pan. Repeat this until the mushrooms are lightly browned on all sides, about 5 minutes total. Don't mix the mushrooms around too much, so they can lightly brown and release any excess liquid. Remove the mushrooms from the pan and set aside.

In the same pan, heat the remaining oil over medium-high heat and add the ginger, garlic, red onion, chiles and Szechuan pepper (if using). Lower the heat to medium and cook for 1 minute, or until the ginger and garlic are aromatic. Add the bell pepper and increase the heat to medium-high. Cook the bell pepper for 2 to 3 minutes, or until tender.

Add the cooked mushrooms back to the pan. Give the sauce a good stir since the starch tends to sit at the bottom. Pour the sauce over the mushrooms and lower the heat to medium. Mix until the sauce coats the mushrooms and starts to thicken. Add the roasted peanuts and mix well. Season with salt to taste. Garnish with chopped scallion, if desired.

Turn off the heat and enjoy while hot with steamed rice.

Umami Bites and Refreshing Salads

These are more than just starters and salads. For me, growing up Asian, appetizers also became somewhat of a side dish, similar to how Koreans enjoy their banchan (side dishes). Starters are an accompaniment to the main dish we'd have served at the dinner table. You could have a Smacked Cucumber Salad (page 142), pieces of crisp and refreshing cucumber soaked in a tangy, savory sauce with a hearty fried rice—this way, the refreshing bite of the cucumber balances out the rich flavors of the rice. Satay Tofu Sticks (page 130)—tofu skewers in a rich coconut milk–based marinade—can be served with steamed jasmine rice, as I've personally enjoyed them. There's really no limit to how you can make a dish and what you can pair them with. You'll discover in this chapter new ways of elevating small bites and techniques to get them to pack that delicious punch of flavor even if they come in small packages.

Chinese Lettuce Wraps (San Choy Bow)

Enjoy these pieces of crunchy lettuce filled with crumbled tofu and mushrooms in a really tasty, savory sauce! This is one of those healthy-yet-delicious starters you can prepare ahead of time and share with your family and friends.

Makes 8 lettuce cups
Prep Time: 20 minutes
Cook Time: 20 minutes

TOFU AND MUSHROOM FILLING

14 oz (400 g) extra-firm tofu

6 fresh shiitake mushrooms

1 tbsp (15 ml) sesame oil

1 small onion, diced

1 clove garlic, minced

½ tsp grated fresh ginger

1 small carrot, diced finely

2 tbsp (30 ml) Chinese Shaoxing wine or dry sherry

STIR-FRY SAUCE

1½ tsp (4 g) cornstarch

1 tbsp (15 ml) vegan oyster sauce (homemade recipe on page 156)

1 tsp sesame oil

1½ tbsp (22 ml) hoisin sauce

2 tbsp (30 ml) room-temperature water

1 tsp dark brown sugar

½ tsp dark soy sauce, for color (optional)

SWEET HOISIN SAUCE (OPTIONAL)

1 tbsp (15 ml) hoisin sauce

3 tbsp (45 ml) water

1½ tsp (8 g) dark brown sugar, or to taste

½ tsp cornstarch

TO SERVE

8 iceberg or romaine lettuce cups

2 tbsp (20 g) crushed peanuts, for topping (optional)

Sliced scallions, for topping (optional)

Sliced bird's eye chile, for topping (optional)

Regular hoisin sauce (optional)

Prepare the filling: Press the tofu for at least 10 minutes to drain any excess liquid (see page 11 for more details). Afterward, place the tofu in a bowl and then crumble with your hands or a fork.

While the tofu is pressing, prepare the stir-fry sauce: In a small bowl, mix all the ingredients until well combined. Set aside.

Slice the shiitake mushrooms into small cubes, about ¼ inch (6 mm) across.

Heat a large skillet or wok over medium heat. Add the oil. Once hot, sauté the onion, garlic and ginger for 2 minutes, or until aromatic. Add the mushrooms and carrot. Increase the heat to high and then pour in the wine. Stir, then cook for 2 to 3 minutes, or until the carrots are tender. Add the mashed tofu and stir-fry sauce, and mix well. Lower the heat to medium-high and continue to cook, stirring about every 2 minutes, until the tofu dries up, resembles minced meat and is lightly browned, about 10 minutes total. Feel free to adjust the seasoning depending on your desired taste. Turn off the heat and transfer the tofu mixture to a bowl. Let cool for 10 minutes before serving.

If using, prepare the sweet hoisin sauce: In a small saucepan, stir together all the sauce ingredients over medium heat. Feel free to adjust the sugar, as some hoisin sauce brands can already contain a significant amount of sugar. Stir until the sauce thickens, 2 minutes, then turn off the heat and set aside.

When ready to eat, place a generous amount of the tofu mixture into each lettuce cup. Top with crushed peanuts, scallions and sliced chile, if desired. Drizzle with the sweet hoisin sauce or just regular hoisin sauce, if desired. Take a bite and enjoy!

Korean Kimchi Pancakes (Kimchi Jeon)

One of the dishes I'd always look forward to when eating at a local Korean restaurant is its kimchi jeon (kimchi pancake). They'd serve kimchi jeon as part of their side dishes (banchan)—it's a great way to use up leftover kimchi and also really quick and simple to prepare. The key here is to use fermented kimchi for the best flavor. I can easily have kimchi pancakes three or four times a week; I make them in big batches and store in the fridge to just reheat in a pan or a toaster oven.

Serves 3
Prep Time: 10 minutes
Cook Time: 20 minutes

PANCAKE BATTER
1 cup + 2 tbsp (140 g) all-purpose flour

3 tbsp (25 g) cornstarch

1¼ cups (300 ml) room-temperature water, plus more if needed

½ cup (120 ml) kimchi juice

1 cup (160 g) vegan kimchi, chopped into 1" (2.5-cm) pieces (homemade recipe on page 158)

3 scallions, sliced (optional)

¼ to ½ tsp salt, or to taste

DIPPING SAUCE
1 tsp cane sugar, or to taste

1 tbsp (15 ml) hot water

1 tbsp (15 ml) soy sauce

1 tbsp (15 ml) rice vinegar

1 tsp toasted sesame oil

½ tsp toasted sesame seeds

Pinch of red pepper flakes or gochugaru (Korean chili powder) (optional)

Chopped scallions (optional)

TO COOK
Neutral oil

Prepare the pancake batter: In a large bowl, combine the flour and cornstarch. Mix well. Slowly pour in the room-temperature water while mixing. Then, add the kimchi juice and mix until you've reached a batter consistency. If the batter is too thick, feel free to add 1 to 2 tablespoons (15 to 30 ml) more of water. Fold in the chopped kimchi and sliced scallions (if using). Mix in ¼ teaspoon of the salt and then taste the batter. If your kimchi isn't very salty and the batter is a bit bland, feel free to add more salt.

Prepare the dipping sauce: In a small bowl, mix together the sugar and hot water until the sugar is dissolved. Add the rest of the sauce ingredients. Mix well and feel free to adjust the seasoning according to your desired taste.

Heat a medium-sized nonstick skillet over medium-high heat. Add enough oil to coat the surface of the pan and let it heat. Pour in ⅓ to ½ cup (80 to 120 ml) of the batter. Note that this will depend on the size of your pan. Evenly spread out the batter and pieces of kimchi until you have a pancake that is ¼ to ½ inch (6 mm to 1.3 cm) thick.

Cook the pancake for 3 to 4 minutes over medium-high heat. Once the sides start to dry up, carefully scrape the sides with a spatula to ensure they haven't stuck to the pan. Once the pancake is crispy and has some brown spots underneath, carefully flip it with a spatula. Cook the other side until browned and crisp, another 3 to 4 minutes. Remove from the pan and repeat this for the rest of the batter.

Transfer the pancakes to a plate or chopping board. You can slice them into smaller pieces before enjoying with dipping sauce!

Satay Tofu Sticks with Peanut Sauce

These are skewers of tofu marinated in a blend of coconut milk and aromatics before being pan-fried and enjoyed with a tasty peanut sauce. This is one of those mouthwatering appetizers you can enjoy with a delicious and refreshing salad.

Makes 6 satay sticks
Prep Time: 20 minutes
Marinate Time: 2 hours
Cook Time: 20 minutes

TOFU AND MARINADE
14 oz (400 g) extra-firm tofu

¼ cup (60 ml) full-fat coconut milk

3 cloves garlic, minced

2 tsp (5 g) grated fresh ginger

1½ tbsp (9 g) curry powder

2 tbsp (30 ml) pure maple syrup

1½ tbsp (22 ml) soy sauce

EQUIPMENT
6 bamboo skewers

PEANUT SAUCE
¼ cup (65 g) smooth peanut butter

2 tbsp (30 ml) warm water

1 tbsp (15 g) coconut sugar, or to taste

1 tbsp (15 ml) rice vinegar

½ tsp minced garlic

½ tsp sesame oil

1½ tsp (8 ml) sriracha or other hot sauce

1 tsp soy sauce

TO COOK
Neutral oil

TO SERVE
Chopped peanuts, for garnish (optional)

Chopped fresh cilantro, for garnish (optional)

Fresh lime wedges

Prepare the tofu: Press the tofu for at least 10 minutes to drain any excess liquid (see page 11 for more details).

In a large, airtight container, mix the marinade ingredients together. Feel free to adjust depending on your desired taste.

Slice the tofu into 1½-inch (3-cm) cubes. Place the tofu in the marinade and flip around to evenly coat with the sauce. Leave the tofu to marinate in the refrigerator for at least 2 hours. You can also leave them to marinate overnight.

Soak the bamboo skewers in warm water for at least 30 minutes to prevent them from burning during cooking.

Prepare the peanut sauce: In a small bowl, mix all the peanut sauce ingredients together until smooth. Feel free to adjust the seasoning and amount of water according to your desired taste and consistency.

After the tofu marinates, place five or six cubes of tofu along each skewer, or as many as you can fit without crowding them.

Cook the skewers: Heat a medium-sized grill pan over medium heat. Brush with a generous amount of oil. Place the tofu skewers on the pan and cook on each side for 4 to 5 minutes, or until lightly charred, pouring the leftover marinade over the tofu for it to absorb while cooking. Once the tofu is lightly charred on all sides, about 15 minutes total, turn off the heat.

Serve the tofu satay sticks with the peanut sauce and top with chopped peanuts, cilantro and a squeeze of fresh lime (if using).

Filipino Pumpkin Fritters (Kalabasa Okoy)

These are thin and crispy pumpkin fritters enjoyed with a sweet chili vinegar dipping sauce. These fritters (okoy) are famous Filipino street food that I grew up eating. They come in different versions—from using shrimp to silverfish—but this is a vegan version made with pumpkin. These are also commonly enjoyed as a delicious and satisfying appetizer and I particularly love them as finger food.

Makes 12 to 14 fritters
Prep Time: 25 minutes
Cook Time: 20 minutes

PUMPKIN FRITTERS

4 cups packed (720 g) grated raw pumpkin or butternut squash (see note)

1 small onion, diced

1 small red bell pepper, seeded and diced

½ cup (65 g) cornstarch

1 cup (125 g) all-purpose flour

1¾ tsp (10 g) salt, or to taste

⅛ tsp freshly ground black pepper

½ cup (120 ml) room-temperature water

Neutral oil, for frying

SWEET CHILI VINEGAR

½ cup (120 ml) distilled white vinegar

½ tsp salt

2 tbsp (30 g) cane sugar, or to taste

¼ tsp freshly ground black pepper

½ medium-sized red onion, diced

1 fresh bird's eye chile, sliced (remove seeds, if desired, for less heat)

Prepare the fritters: In a large bowl, combine the pumpkin, onion and bell pepper and mix well. In a medium-sized bowl, combine the cornstarch, flour, salt and black pepper. While stirring with a spatula, add the flour mixture to the pumpkin mixture. Mix everything together until the vegetables are coated in the flour mixture. Carefully pour in the water and then mix until the fritter mixture is well incorporated and holds up well. If you find that the mixture is too wet and doesn't hold very well, you can add 1 to 2 tablespoons (8 to 16 g) more of all-purpose flour. The pumpkin may naturally release liquid as time passes, due to the salt.

Heat a large skillet over medium-high heat. Add enough oil to submerge the fritters.

Meanwhile, prepare the sweet chili vinegar: In a small bowl, mix together all the sauce ingredients until the sugar is dissolved.

Once the oil is hot and bubbling, scoop about ½ cup (120 g) of the mixture and then flatten it on your palm until it's about ½ inch (1.3 cm) thick. Carefully slide the fritter into the oil. You can continue to flatten the fritters once submerged in the oil by using a spatula. Fry on each side for 3 minutes, or until golden brown and crisp on the edges. Flip over and fry the other side as well for another 3 minutes.

Once the fritters are crisp throughout, remove them from the oil and transfer to a strainer to drain any excess oil. Don't cover them while still hot, to prevent them from becoming soggy. After cooking the rest of the fritters, turn off the heat. Serve the fritters hot with the chili vinegar on the side for dipping.

Note: To grate your pumpkin or squash, slice it in half and remove the seeds. Slice into wedges and then carefully peel off the skin, using a peeler. To grate, you can use a cheese grater.

Curry Tofu Cakes

You'll love biting into these cakes of tofu seasoned with curry powder, ginger and cilantro, with a kick of spice from the chiles. You can enjoy these curry cakes with your favorite sweet chili sauce as is or with Vermicelli Noodle Salad (page 141) on the side for a really tasty start to your meal.

Makes 15 cakes
Prep Time: 15 minutes
Cook Time: 20 minutes

14 oz (400 g) extra-firm tofu

⅓ cup (45 g) finely grated carrot

2 bird's eye chiles, sliced (optional)

2 tbsp (2 g) chopped fresh cilantro

2 tbsp (14 g) curry powder

1¼ (7 g) tsp sea salt

½ large green or red bell pepper, seeded and diced

½ tsp minced fresh ginger

1 tsp minced garlic

½ cup (65 g) all-purpose flour, plus more if needed

¼ tsp freshly ground black pepper

Neutral oil, for frying

Sweet chili sauce or the dipping sauce of your choice, for serving

Press the tofu for at least 10 minutes to drain any excess liquid (see page 11 for more details). Afterward, place the tofu in a bowl and crumble with your hands or a fork. Add the carrot, chiles (if using), cilantro, curry powder, salt, bell pepper, ginger, garlic, flour and black pepper. Mix everything together until well incorporated.

Scoop a golf ball–sized amount of the tofu mixture and then carefully shape it into small patties that are 1 inch (2.5 cm) thick. Repeat this for the remaining mixture. If the mixture is too wet and doesn't hold up well, feel free to add 1 to 2 tablespoons (8 to 16 g) more of all-purpose flour.

Heat a large, nonstick pan or skillet over high heat. Add enough oil to cover the surface of the pan. Once the oil is hot and has small bubbles, carefully place each patty into the pan. You may need to do this in batches if all of them do not fit in your pan. Lower the heat to medium-high and fry the patties for 5 to 6 minutes on the first side, or until they are golden brown. Flip the patties and then repeat for the remaining side. Once golden brown and crisp, remove the patties from the oil and transfer to a strainer or a paper towel–lined plate to drain any excess oil.

Serve the cakes hot and enjoy with your favorite sweet chili sauce or dipping sauce of choice.

Vietnamese Sizzling Crepes (Bánh Xèo)

I first tried bánh xèo after a boat ride through the Mekong Delta, where we stopped at a floating restaurant for lunch. For a veganized version of this dish, they added lots of bean sprouts to the crepe instead of the usual pork and shrimp. They served the bánh xèo with rice paper and a plate full of herbs and vegetables, so you could wrap it on your own before dipping it into the sauce. This is a slightly different version, where I added some mushrooms and wrapped it in lettuce. Each bite is deliciously savory and refreshing, and you really have to use your hands to get that full experience.

Makes 5 crepes
Prep Time: 15 minutes
Cook Time: 25 minutes

FILLING

1 tbsp (15 ml) neutral oil

9 oz (250 g) fresh bean sprouts

9 oz (250 g) fresh mushrooms of choice, such as shiitake, oyster and button

2 tbsp (30 ml) vegan fish sauce, or to taste (homemade recipe on page 161)

CREPE BATTER

¾ cup (80 g) rice flour

¼ cup (30 g) all-purpose flour

1 tsp ground turmeric

¼ tsp sea salt

1¼ cups (300 ml) room-temperature water

⅔ cup (160 ml) room-temperature full-fat coconut cream

1 scallion, finely chopped

Neutral oil, for cooking

TO SERVE

¼ cup (60 ml) vegan fish sauce

1½ tsp (8 g) coconut or palm sugar, or to taste

1 tbsp (15 ml) fresh lime juice

1 head of lettuce

Handful of fresh mint, cilantro and Thai basil leaves

Prepare the filling: Heat a 10-inch (25-cm) nonstick skillet over high heat. Once hot, add the oil. Sauté the bean sprouts and mushrooms until tender, 3 to 4 minutes. Add the fish sauce to taste, mix, then transfer to a small bowl. Set aside.

Prepare the crepe batter: In a medium-sized bowl, combine the rice flour, all-purpose flour, turmeric and salt. Stir together until well incorporated. While mixing with a spatula, pour in the water, coconut cream and scallion. Mix the batter until smooth.

Heat the same pan used for the vegetables over high heat. Do not add oil. Once the pan smokes and is hot, add one-fifth of the mushrooms and bean sprouts and spread evenly on the pan. Give the batter a good stir. Carefully lift the pan from the heat, scoop ½ cup (120 ml) of batter from the bowl, then pour it into the pan while turning the pan clockwise slightly to spread the batter. The batter will sizzle! If there are uncovered spots, add 1 to 2 tablespoons (15 to 30 ml) of the batter to cover the spots.

Place the pan back on the stove and then lower the heat to medium. Cover the pan and then leave the crepe to cook for 4 minutes, or until the sides of the crepe start to crisp and lift off the pan. Brush oil on the sides of the crepe, then cook for another 2 minutes, or until the crepe has brown spots underneath. Carefully fold the crepe in half. You don't need to flip and cook the other side. Slide the crepe from the pan onto a plate. Repeat this for the rest of the vegetables and batter.

While the crepes cook, prepare the dipping sauce: In a small bowl, mix together the vegan fish sauce, sugar and lime juice until the sugar dissolves. Feel free to adjust the measurements to your desired taste.

To enjoy the bánh xèo, slice a small piece of crepe and add it to a lettuce leaf along with fresh herbs. Wrap the lettuce, dip it in the sauce, then take a bite!

Seaweed and Cucumber Salad with Miso-Sesame Dressing

This salad is inspired by Japanese sunomono, or vinegar-based dishes, which I love to have as starters in Japanese restaurants. Sunomono usually features cucumber marinated in vinegar. This version uses a mix of wakame, a kind of seaweed, and cucumber in a sweet and slightly sour dressing that's packed with umami from the miso. This salad is incredibly easy and healthy at the same time!

Serves 2
Prep Time: 20 minutes
Cook Time: None

SEAWEED AND CUCUMBER SALAD

1 large cucumber

1½ tsp (11 g) coarse salt

2 tbsp (10 g) dried wakame (makes 3.5 oz [100 g] once rehydrated)

MISO-SESAME DRESSING

1 tbsp (25 g) white miso paste

1½ tbsp (22 ml) rice vinegar

2 tsp (8 g) cane sugar, or to taste

1 tsp toasted sesame oil

1 tsp toasted sesame seeds, plus more for topping

Prepare the salad: Cut off and discard both ends of the cucumber. Slice the cucumber into thin strips, about ¼ inch (6 mm) thick. Place the sliced cucumber in a colander set over a bowl to catch the liquid underneath. Add the coarse salt and mix well with the cucumber. Leave the cucumber to sit for at least 10 minutes to drain any excess liquid. This step is essential so the cucumber doesn't release its liquid when mixed with the dressing later on. Stir the cucumber after the first 5 minutes to ensure that all the pieces are coated in the salt. After at least 10 minutes, squeeze out the excess liquid from the cucumber.

While the cucumber is in the salt mixture, place the dried seaweed in a medium-sized heatproof bowl. Pour in enough boiling hot water to completely submerge the seaweed and then leave the seaweed to rehydrate for at least 5 minutes. Remove the seaweed from the water and then squeeze out any excess liquid. Set aside.

Run the cucumber under cold water to wash off the salt. Squeeze out the excess liquid.

Prepare the dressing: In a large bowl or container, mix together the dressing ingredients. Feel free to add more vinegar or sugar, depending on your desired sourness and sweetness. Add the cucumber and rehydrated seaweed, then mix everything well until the cucumber and seaweed are coated in the dressing. Top the salad with more sesame seeds, if desired.

Refrigerate the salad for at least 30 minutes for it to absorb the flavors. This salad is best consumed cold. It can be kept in the refrigerator for up to 3 days until ready to eat.

Vermicelli Noodle Salad

Here's a really refreshing noodle salad with fresh, crunchy veggies and fragrant herbs in a light yet tasty dressing! This is one of those really easy salads to prepare that's perfect as a side or appetizer along with barbecue or other dishes, such as Satay Tofu Sticks (page 130), Crispy Vegetable Egg Rolls (page 18) or even dumplings.

Serves 3
Prep Time: 20 minutes
Cook Time: None

NOODLES

1.8 oz (50 g) dried glass (mung bean) noodles or rice vermicelli

Boiling water, to cook noodles

DRESSING

2 tbsp (30 ml) soy sauce

2 tbsp (30 ml) rice vinegar

2 tsp (10 g) coconut sugar or other sugar of choice

1 tbsp (15 ml) neutral oil

1 garlic clove, minced

1 bird's eye chile, thinly sliced (optional)

SALAD

1 cup (75 g) shredded cabbage

½ small red bell pepper, thinly sliced

1 small carrot, peeled and thinly sliced

1 green onion, thinly sliced

1 tbsp (1 g) packed finely chopped fresh cilantro leaves, plus more for garnish

1 tbsp (1 g) packed finely chopped fresh mint leaves

2 tbsp (15 g) chopped roasted peanuts, plus more for garnish (optional)

Prepare the noodles: Place the noodles in a heatproof bowl. Pour boiling water into the bowl until the noodles are completely submerged. Let cook for 6 to 7 minutes, or until chewy and cooked through. Drain the excess liquid and let the noodles cool. Using scissors or a knife, roughly cut the noodles into bite-sized pieces, about 2 inches (5 cm) in length.

Prepare the dressing: In a small bowl or jar, combine all the dressing ingredients. Mix or shake to incorporate everything. Taste the dressing and feel free to adjust the sweetness and tanginess, as desired. Set aside.

Assemble the salad: In a large bowl, combine the vegetables, herbs and peanuts (if using) along with the sliced noodles. Pour the dressing over everything and then mix together until well incorporated. Refrigerate the salad for at least 30 minutes. Top with more chopped cilantro and peanuts, if desired. This salad is best enjoyed cold and will continue to absorb the flavors of the dressing. It can be stored in the refrigerator for up to 3 days.

Smacked Cucumber Salad

This is a simple yet really refreshing and flavorful salad with cucumbers that are smacked instead of sliced—resulting in uneven cuts and a unique texture. The cucumbers are soaked in a light, tasty and refreshing dressing that gets better over time as the cucumbers absorb it. This is best prepared in advance for optimal flavor.

Serves 2
Prep Time: 20 minutes
Cook Time: None

2 medium-sized kirby cucumbers

¾ tsp salt

3 cloves garlic, minced

¾ tsp cane sugar, or to taste

1 tbsp (15 ml) light soy sauce

2 tsp (10 ml) sesame oil

1 tsp toasted sesame seeds

1 tsp rice vinegar

1 tsp chili-garlic oil with sediment (optional; homemade recipe on page 157)

Cut the ends off each cucumber. Place both cucumbers on a chopping board or any flat surface. Smack the cucumbers a few times with a rolling pin or the flat blade of a cleaver to split them. Afterward, slice each cucumber lengthwise into four pieces, then diagonally into 1-inch (2.5-cm)-thick slices.

Place the cucumber in a strainer with a bowl underneath. Sprinkle the cucumbers with the salt and mix well. Set the cucumber aside for at least 15 minutes to release the excess liquid. You can opt to rinse the cucumbers under running water two or three times to wash off the salt, or set them aside and add them directly to the sauce if you want saltier cucumbers. Drain the bowl that had been beneath the strainer.

In that same bowl, combine the garlic, sugar, soy sauce, sesame oil and seeds, vinegar and chili-garlic oil (if using) in the bowl. Mix everything together, taste and then adjust the seasoning depending on your preference. Add the cucumbers to the mixture and toss everything together until the cucumbers are well coated.

This is best enjoyed after the cucumber has been refrigerated and marinated in the mixture for at least 30 minutes. It can be stored in the refrigerator for up to 3 days.

Tempting Sweets and Treats

This chapter is composed of a few of my favorite desserts or sweet treats. From the iconic Thai Mango Sticky Rice (page 148)—glutinous rice cooked down in a rich coconut sauce—to Filipino Caramelized Banana Rolls (page 146), better known as turon in the Philippines, this section is short but really sweet. You'll find that these are desserts you can enjoy not just to end your meals, but as the perfect snack to have during merienda or with your afternoon tea or coffee.

Filipino Caramelized Banana Rolls (Turon)

Turon is deemed the pambansang merienda—the country's afternoon snack—in the Philippines. It's sold by a lot of street vendors, as something you can enjoy for dessert after lunch or for merienda. It's pieces of banana inside flour wrappers, fried to a crisp with sugar to create that delicious caramelized coating. As it makes use of really simple ingredients, it's normally sold for only 20 pesos (that's a little less than $0.50!). Turon is commonly made with small, plump Saba or Cardava bananas, which grow locally in that country. For this version, I make use of plantains that still achieve the same flavor with a slightly different texture, but overall are still really satisfying!

Makes 8 rolls
Prep Time: 10 minutes
Cook Time: 20 minutes

8 flour spring roll or lumpia wrappers, thawed at room temperature if frozen

4 medium-sized ripe plantains or regular bananas, 7" (17.5 cm) in length (see note)

3 tbsp (45 g) dark brown sugar or coconut sugar

TO COOK AND SERVE
Neutral oil, for frying

5 to 6 tbsp (65 to 80 g) dark brown sugar or coconut sugar

Vegan vanilla ice cream (optional)

Note: If you have access to Saba or Cardava bananas, which are what's usually used for turon, that would be even better! You can use a total of 8 Saba or Cardava bananas and halve them to use one for each roll, since these bananas are smaller.

If using regular bananas, make sure they are still firm. Do not use overripe bananas as they will turn out very mushy.

Carefully separate the wrappers from one another. Cover them with a clean, damp towel to prevent them from drying out.

Without peeling it, chop off both ends of a plantain before slicing it in half lengthwise. Remove the peel and place the plantain halves on a plate. Repeat for the remaining plantains.

Spread the brown sugar on a large, shallow bowl or plate. Dip each plantain in the sugar and coat evenly.

Place a flour wrapper on a flat surface. If using a square wrapper, place it diagonally away from you so it creates a diamond shape. Prepare a small bowl of water to seal the edges of the wrapper. Transfer a sugar-coated plantain half horizontally on the center of the spring roll wrapper.

Fold the bottom end of the wrapper toward the center of the wrapper, away from you, to cover the plantain half with it, then press down to compress. Dip your finger into the bowl of water, then dab the left and right pointed edges of the wrapper with water and fold them to the center. Press down to seal the wet wrapper over the plantain half. From there, continue to roll the wrapper to the topmost pointed edge of the wrapper and seal it with water before rolling it over to conceal any edges of the fold beneath the wrapped roll.

Transfer the wrapped roll to a plate and cover with a clean towel to prevent it from drying out. Repeat this step for the rest of the plantain and wrappers until you have 8 rolls.

Cook the rolls: Heat a large skillet or wok over high heat. Add enough oil to submerge the rolls at least halfway. Once the oil is hot, add the brown sugar. The sugar will bubble and melt due to the heat of the oil. Mix it around with a spatula to prevent it from sticking to

the pan. Add about four rolls—note that this will depend on the size of your pan. Lower the heat to medium-high and cook the rolls for 2 minutes on each side, or until golden brown, moving them around in the melted sugar every 30 seconds to evenly coat the wrapper. Flip over the rolls to brown on the remaining side for another 2 minutes, scooping up the melted sugar onto the rolls, if needed, to evenly coat the rolls.

Carefully remove the rolls from the oil and transfer to a strainer to quickly drain away any excess oil before transferring them to a flat plate or tray to cool. The sugar will continue to harden as it cools after cooking. Do not place the coated rolls on paper towels, as the sugar will stick. Properly space apart the cooked rolls and ensure they don't stick to one another, since the sugar is

sticky while still hot. Leave the rolls to cool for 5 minutes or until the sugar has hardened. Do not cover the rolls as they will get soggy. Repeat the process to cook and cool the remaining rolls.

These are best enjoyed when freshly cooked and the outer caramel coating and wrapper are still crisp. You can enjoy them as is, or with a scoop of vegan vanilla ice cream.

Thai Mango Sticky Rice

This is probably one of my favorite desserts. It takes me back to eating this by the roadside in Bangkok and sharing it with my sister, who loves it, too! It's a delicious combination of glutinous rice cooked in coconut milk along with fresh sweet ripe mangoes. It's actually also really simple to make at home!

Serves 4
Prep Time: 15 minutes
Cook Time: 40 minutes

COCONUT RICE
1 cup (210 g) uncooked glutinous rice
1 cup (240 ml) full-fat coconut milk
¼ cup (55 g) cane sugar
½ tsp sea salt

COCONUT SAUCE
½ cup (120 ml) full-fat coconut milk
3 tbsp (45 g) granulated sugar
1 tsp cornstarch
2 tsp (10 ml) room-temperature water

MANGOES
2 large ripe mangoes
Toasted sesame seeds, for topping

Prepare the coconut rice: Wash the rice three times, then leave it to soak in room-temperature water for at least 8 hours and up to 24 hours. Afterward, drain the water from the rice. Line a bamboo steamer with parchment paper on the bottom and up at the sides, to prevent the rice from sticking to the steamer. If using a regular steamer with a metal or glass lid, line that steamer with parchment paper and wrap its lid with a large kitchen cloth so it can absorb the excess liquid. Place the rice in the prepared steamer and steam it for 25 to 30 minutes, or until the rice is chewy. The cooked rice grains will turn translucent.

In a large pan, heat the coconut milk over medium-high heat. Add the sugar and salt. Bring the coconut milk to a boil, about 3 minutes, stirring the mixture every 30 seconds.

Once it boils, lower the heat to medium and then continue to stir until the sugar has dissolved. Add the steamed rice and stir well into the coconut milk mixture. Cook down the rice until it has absorbed the coconut milk and thickened, about 4 minutes. Turn off the heat, transfer the rice into a medium-sized bowl and let cool for 5 minutes.

Prepare the coconut sauce: In the same pan, over medium-high heat, add the coconut milk and sugar. Lower the heat to medium, stir in the same direction and cook until the mixture boils, about 2 minutes, then lower the heat to low.

Meanwhile, in a small bowl stir together the cornstarch and room-temperature water. While stirring the sauce, pour in the cornstarch mixture. Turn off the heat and keep stirring until it thickens, about 1 minute. Transfer to a small bowl until ready to use.

Peel the mangoes and then carefully slice from the topmost part all the way to the bottom, while following the seed, to create a total of four halves. Slice each mango half into ½-inch (1.3-cm)-thick strips. Portion the rice and the sliced mangoes into four servings, then top with the toasted sesame seeds. Finish them off by drizzling with some of the coconut sauce. This is best enjoyed when freshly made.

Storage and Reheating Tips

You can refrigerate the servings overnight if you have leftovers, though they should be consumed within a day or 2 days at most, because coconut cream can easily go bad.

When you refrigerate these, the rice will harden. If you want to enjoy them as they were when freshly made, transfer the rice in a microwave-safe container, then sprinkle some water on the rice. Cover it and then microwave for 30 to 45 seconds so the rice can cook in the steam.

Matcha Cookies

These matcha cookies feature that distinct flavor and color from the matcha that really complements the subtle sweetness of the cookies. These can also be made crisp or chewy by adjusting the baking time. They're perfect enjoyed as is or with your favorite tea or drink.

Makes 12 cookies
Prep Time: 20 minutes
Bake Time: 20 minutes

FLAX "EGG"
1 tbsp (12 g) flaxseed meal
2 tbsp (30 ml) room-temperature water

DRY INGREDIENTS
1 cup (125 g) all-purpose flour
½ tsp baking soda
¼ tsp sea salt
1½ to 2 tsp (4 to 5 g) matcha powder, adjust according to your desired flavor

WET INGREDIENTS
¼ cup (60 ml) neutral oil
½ cup (110 g) cane sugar
2 tbsp (30 ml) room-temperature soy or oat milk
½ tsp vanilla extract

Prepare the flax "egg": In a small bowl, mix together the flaxseed meal and water. Let sit in the refrigerator for 5 minutes, or until it thickens.

Preheat your oven to 375°F (190°C). Line a baking sheet with a silicone mat or parchment paper.

Prepare the dry ingredients: In a large bowl, whisk together the dry ingredients until well incorporated. Ensure that there are no clumps of baking soda.

Prepare the wet ingredients: In a separate medium-sized bowl, mix together the oil and sugar with a spatula until well incorporated. Add the flax egg, milk and vanilla extract, then mix well. Set aside.

Create a well in the center of the dry ingredients. Slowly pour the wet mixture into the dry mixture. Mix well using a spatula until well incorporated and no dry flour is visible. This will be a really thick cookie dough.

Form the cookie dough into balls by scooping 2 tablespoons (28 g) of the dough. Shape each into a ball and place each ball 3 inches (7.5 cm) apart on the baking sheet before flattening each to about 2 inches (5 cm) in diameter.

For chewy cookies, bake the cookies for 12 minutes, remove from the oven, transfer to a wire rack and let cool for another 10 minutes, as they will continue to harden.

For crisp cookies, bake the cookies for 15 to 16 minutes, remove from the oven and let cool on a wire rack for another 10 minutes, as they will continue to harden.

You can store the cookies in an airtight container at room temperature for up to 3 days, or they can be stored in the refrigerator for up to 1 week.

Coconut Cupcakes

These mini coconut cupcakes are inspired by Filipino coconut macaroons and puto (steamed rice cakes). These cupcakes are light, moist, fluffy and cakelike, but not too sweet! They're packed with a delicious coconut flavor, with an added bite from the dried shreds. I also added some pandan extract for a layer of fragrance with its vanilla-like aroma and hint of coconut; I love to use it in both sweet and savory recipes. This recipe makes a quick batch that you can easily double for more cupcakes!

Makes 9 cupcakes
Prep Time: 15 minutes
Bake Time: 25 minutes

¾ cup (180 ml) room-temperature soy or oat milk

½ tsp distilled white vinegar

1 cup (125 g) all-purpose flour

¼ tsp baking powder

⅛ tsp baking soda

¼ tsp sea salt

½ cup (45 g) dried unsweetened desiccated coconut shreds

3 tbsp (45 ml) melted coconut oil

5 tbsp (75 g) cane sugar

¼ cup (60 ml) full-fat coconut milk

¼ tsp pandan extract or powder, for extra flavor (optional)

Toasted coconut chips or more desiccated coconut, for topping

Preheat your oven to 350°F (180°C). Place a liner in nine wells of a muffin tin.

In a medium-sized bowl, combine the soy milk and vinegar. Set aside and let curdle for 5 minutes.

In a separate medium-sized bowl, whisk together the flour, baking powder, baking soda, salt and desiccated coconut. Ensure that there are no clumps of baking soda.

Add the coconut oil, sugar, coconut milk and pandan extract or powder (if using) to the soy milk mixture and mix until well incorporated. Create a well in the center of the dry ingredients. Pour the wet mixture into the dry mixture while stirring together with a spatula. Fold together the dry and wet ingredients until no dry flour is visible. Do not overmix the batter. Lumps are totally fine!

Divide the batter equally among your cupcake liners. I used 2½-inch (6.3-cm) cupcake liners and filled each of them three-quarters full with 2 heaping tablespoons (35 ml) of the mixture.

Bake the cupcakes for 20 to 25 minutes, or until a toothpick inserted into the center of a cupcake comes out clean. Remove the cupcakes from the tin and transfer to a wire rack. Allow the cupcakes to cool for a few minutes before topping with the extra coconut and serving. You can store these cupcakes at room temperature for up to 2 days and in the refrigerators for up to 1 week.

Make Your Own Basics and Sauces

This chapter contains simple, easy-to-make basics that I always have stored in my pantry or refrigerator. From homemade vegan kimchi (page 158) all the way to teriyaki sauce (page 160), these basics are some that you can easily prepare yourself to use for various recipes and dishes. Not only are they extremely handy to have readily made to use, but you'll also save up a lot from having to purchase them and will be able to adjust the flavors according to how you'd like them!

Vegan Mushroom "Oyster" Sauce

This is a homemade vegan version of oyster sauce that's deliciously savory with umami from mushrooms. It's slightly thicker and less salty than regular store-bought vegan mushroom "oyster" sauce and stir-fry sauces, but adds a nice depth of flavor to recipes.

Makes 1¼ cups (295 ml) sauce

Prep Time: 20 minutes

Cook Time: 10 minutes

1 oz (28 g) dried shiitake mushrooms (about 10 pieces)

1½ cups (360 ml) boiling water

½ tsp minced garlic

¼ cup packed (56 g) dark brown sugar, or according to desired sweetness

¼ cup (60 ml) soy sauce

Place the dried mushrooms in a large, heatproof bowl. Pour in the boiling water. Cover the mushrooms and let sit for 15 minutes, or until they are plump and rehydrated. Do not discard the water.

Transfer the mushrooms and mushroom water to a blender. Blend everything until completely smooth.

Place the pureed mushrooms in a saucepan and add the rest of the ingredients. Mix well and simmer over medium heat until the sugar has melted completely, about 3 minutes. Feel free to adjust the seasoning based on your desired taste.

Turn off the heat, then let the sauce cool completely before transferring to an airtight container or jar. Store in the refrigerator for up to 2 months.

Chili-Garlic Oil

This chili-garlic oil is a blend of fresh garlic and chiles cooked down with additional spices. It's packed full of flavor and gives that delicious kick of spice and extra depth of flavor to a dish! The oil and sediment are also delicious to be used in your dipping sauce for dumplings and as an added layer of flavor to your stir-fries.

Makes 1 cup (240 ml) sauce
Prep Time: 5 minutes
Cook Time: 25 minutes

2 oz (55 g) bird's eye chiles (about 30 pieces)
12 cloves garlic, peeled
¾ cup (180 ml) neutral oil
½ tsp salt
1 tsp cane sugar
¼ tsp Chinese five-spice powder
1 dried bay leaf (optional)
1 whole dried star anise (optional)
1 tsp Szechuan peppercorns, crushed or ground (optional)

Chop off the top ends and stem of the chiles. Then, place the chiles and garlic cloves in a food processor. Process until the chile and garlic are minced.

Heat a medium-sized saucepan over medium-high heat. Add the neutral oil along with the salt, sugar and Chinese five-spice powder. Add the bay leaf, star anise and Szechuan peppercorns (if using).

Lower the heat to medium and simmer the oil mixture for 5 minutes, then add the minced garlic and chiles. Cook everything over medium heat, stirring every 2 to 3 minutes, until the chiles have turned into a much darker shade of red, about 20 minutes total.

Turn off the heat, then let the mixture cool completely before storing. Store the chili-garlic oil in an airtight container or jar in a cool, dark place for up to 3 months.

Vegan Kimchi

This easy vegan kimchi is packed full of flavor with a crisp, tangy and spicy kick. It's a staple at home and I always have a batch in the refrigerator to enjoy as a side dish (banchan) or for Korean Kimchi Pancakes (page 129) or Korean Kimchi Stew (page 84).

Makes 4 cups (850 g) kimchi

Prep Time: 20 minutes

Soak Time: 2 hours

CABBAGE
1 (1½-lb [670-g]) head napa cabbage
¼ cup (75 g) coarse salt
½ cup (120 ml) room-temperature water

KIMCHI PASTE
½ cup (120 ml) room-temperature water
4 tsp (13 g) glutinous rice flour (see notes)
1 tbsp (15 g) cane sugar
5 cloves garlic
1 small knob fresh ginger, peeled
⅓ cup (33 g) gochugaru (Korean chili powder)
1 small white onion, quartered

ADD-INS
½ medium-sized carrot, thinly julienned
1 cup (50 g) thinly sliced scallion
1 tsp salt (optional; see notes)

Prepare the Cabbage

Slice the napa cabbage in half, and then into quarters. Cut away the tough cores, then slice the cabbage into 2-inch (5-cm)-thick strips. Place the sliced cabbage in a large bowl.

Sprinkle with the coarse salt and pour in the water. Stir the cabbage to evenly coat with the salt mixture.

Let the cabbage sit in the salt water mixture for at least 1½ hours, stirring every 30 minutes to evenly coat in the salt mixture.

At the end of the 1½ hours, rinse the cabbage two or three times under running water to remove excess salt and any dirt. Drain the cabbage and squeeze out the liquid. If you want lots of juice in your kimchi after fermentation, leave a little of the excess liquid to be released when fermenting. More fermentation tips to follow.

Place the drained cabbage back in its large bowl.

Prepare the Kimchi Paste

Heat a small saucepan over medium-low heat. Add the water and then stir in the glutinous rice flour. Increase the heat to medium.

Stir continuously until the flour mixture has turned into a very thick paste. Turn off the heat and then let cool for a few minutes.

Place the flour paste, sugar, garlic, ginger, gochugaru and onion in a blender or food processor. Blend or process until the paste is well incorporated.

Mix the Kimchi

Add the carrot and sliced scallion to the drained cabbage. Add the kimchi paste and mix until well incorporated. Add the salt, to taste, if needed, and mix well.

Divide the kimchi among jars or airtight containers. Tightly pack the kimchi by pressing it down with a spoon, ensuring that you do not fill the jars or containers to the brim, as kimchi will expand as it ferments—fill the jars only three-quarters full.

Fermentation Process

Leave the kimchi to ferment in the jars or airtight containers at room temperature for at least 24 to 48 hours. Do not open your bottle of kimchi for the first 24 hours. The fermentation time will vary depending on your room temperature. This may take a little over 2 days in colder climates. Fermentation is faster in warmer room temperatures. Fermentation gives kimchi the sour taste and as it continues to ferment, the sour taste and smell strengthens, and so does the flavor of the kimchi.

Notes and FAQ

Flour—Glutinous rice flour is what's traditionally used. If you don't have access to it, feel free to use regular rice flour or even all-purpose flour.

Salt—Seasoning with salt is sometimes unnecessary, since the cabbage is soaked in salt water and absorbs the salt over time. It would be best to taste the kimchi first before seasoning with salt. You can always add the salt even a few days after when flavors start to infuse and strengthen.

Too salty?—If your kimchi becomes too salty after fermenting, you can add more vegetables, such as sliced carrots, scallion or radish, to absorb the saltiness. Let it sit in the refrigerator and try it again after a few days.

More Fermentation Tips

Bubbles and air pockets—You'll notice that the kimchi will expand and form bubbles during fermentation. This is a good sign!

After fermentation—After the kimchi has fermented and you're happy with how sour it is, give it a good stir to make sure all the veggies are soaked in the liquid. Compress the kimchi again and pack it tightly before sealing the container, then place it in the refrigerator to keep it fresh for longer.

Kimchi juice—Kimchi juice is perfect to use in certain recipes, such as Korean Kimchi Stew (page 84) and Korean Kimchi Pancakes (page 129), because it definitely adds to the color and the taste. But what if your kimchi doesn't have too much liquid? I find that squeezing the cabbage too much during the preparation process takes out a lot of its liquid, so even after fermentation, it no longer releases so much water to create a lot of juice. If you want juicy kimchi, you can just wash the cabbage well to remove the salt and not squeeze it too dry before mixing in the paste.

Storage—Kimchi can last for really long in the refrigerator, though I can't give an exact time frame! The flavors do get stronger as it sits in the juices longer, so it's important to take note of that, especially if your kimchi is a bit salty at the start.

Teriyaki Sauce

This is an authentic teriyaki sauce, made with only four ingredients, and it has that perfect balance of sweet and savory. You can also opt to thicken this into a glaze to use as a dip or coat your favorite dishes with. Traditional teriyaki sauce is actually made without starches, since it slightly thickens from the sweetener and sugars from the sake and mirin.

Makes 1 cup (240 ml) sauce

Prep Time: 5 minutes

Cook Time: 10 minutes

TERIYAKI SAUCE

½ cup (120 ml) sake

½ cup (120 ml) hon mirin or mirin

½ cup (120 ml) soy sauce

¼ cup (55 g) dark brown sugar or cane sugar, or to taste

GLAZE (OPTIONAL)

1½ tbsp (12 g) cornstarch

3 tbsp (45 ml) room-temperature water

Heat a medium-sized saucepan over medium heat. Add the sake, mirin, soy sauce and sugar. Simmer over medium-high heat until the mixture starts to boil. Continue to stir the sauce in one direction until the sugar has completely dissolved.

Let the sauce boil over medium-high heat until it starts to slightly thicken from the sugars, 7 to 8 minutes.

If making the sauce into a glaze, prepare a cornstarch slurry by stirring the cornstarch and water together in a small bowl. While mixing, pour the slurry into the teriyaki sauce and let boil until the sauce thickens, about 2 minutes. Once it thickens, taste the sauce and adjust the seasonings accordingly.

Turn off the heat. The sauce will continue to thicken as it cools. Transfer the sauce to a jar and let cool completely before storing. It can be stored in the refrigerator for up to 1 month.

Vegan Fish Sauce

This is a really simple homemade vegan "fish" sauce perfect for Southeast Asian dishes, such as Pad Thai (page 46), Vietnamese Bành Xéo (page 137) and more!

Makes 1 cup (240 ml) sauce
Prep Time: 10 minutes
Cook Time: None

¼ cup (55 g) coconut sugar
1 tsp red pepper flakes
1 tsp minced fresh garlic
¾ cup (180 ml) boiling water
2 tbsp (30 ml) fresh lime juice
1½ to 2 tsp (9 to 12 g) sea salt

In a small, heatproof bowl, combine the sugar, red pepper flakes and garlic. Pour in the boiling water. Mix well until the sugar has dissolved. Add the lime juice and salt—you can start with the least amount of salt and just add more depending on your desired saltiness level.

Let the sauce cool before storing in an airtight container. Store in the refrigerator for up to 3 weeks. The flavors will get stronger as it sits.

Homemade Sweet Soy Sauce (Kecap Manis)

This is a homemade sweet, syrupy and thick soy sauce perfect to use for such dishes as Indonesian Fried Rice (page 38). It's also perfect to use as a sauce base for tofu and vegetables.

Makes 1 cup (240 ml) sauce
Prep Time: 5 minutes
Cook Time: 15 minutes

1 cup (240 ml) soy sauce
1 cup (220 g) brown sugar
2 whole dried star anise
4 cloves garlic, halved or crushed
1 (1" [2.5-cm]) piece fresh ginger
1 tsp whole black peppercorns

In a saucepan over medium-low heat, stir together all the ingredients. Cook for about 15 minutes, stirring occasionally, until the sugar has dissolved and the sauce has thickened. If the sauce comes to a boil at any point, lower the heat so that it remains at a low simmer.

Turn off the heat. Remove or strain out the garlic, star anise, ginger and peppercorns. Let the mixture cool. The sweet soy sauce will continue to thicken as it cools.

Store in an airtight container in the refrigerator for up to 6 months.

Ginger and Scallion Sauce

Here's a really fragrant and aromatic sauce that's so versatile. Enjoy it as your favorite condiment or dipping sauce, top it over steamed rice, include it in your stir-fries . . . the list is endless!

Makes 1½ cups (355 ml) sauce
Prep Time: 5 minutes
Cook Time: 5 minutes

4 oz (115 g) scallions, white parts included

2 oz (55 g) fresh ginger

¾ to 1 tsp salt, or to taste

⅛ tsp Chinese five-spice powder (optional)

¾ cup (180 ml) neutral oil (see note)

Remove the bottom root end of the scallions. Slice the scallions into 2-inch (5-cm)-long pieces. Peel the ginger and then slice into 1-inch (2.5-cm) pieces. Place the chopped scallions and ginger in a food processor and process until they are minced.

Place the scallions and ginger in a large, heatproof bowl. Add the salt and Chinese five-spice powder (if using) and mix well.

In a small saucepan or pot, heat the oil over high heat for 3 to 4 minutes, or until it starts to bubble and a piece of scallion sizzles when you add it. Turn off the heat.

Immediately and carefully, pour the sizzling hot oil into your bowl of ginger and scallions. Carefully mix everything together with a heatproof spoon. Taste the mixture and add more salt to taste, if needed. Mix well.

Let the mixture cool completely before transferring to an airtight jar. Make sure that all the ginger and scallion pieces are submerged in the oil. The sauce can be stored in the refrigerator for up to 1 month.

Note: Using a neutral oil is essential as other types of oil, such as olive oil or coconut oil, will completely overpower the flavors of the ginger and scallion.

Acknowledgments

First and foremost, I want to thank everyone at Page Street Publishing. To the publisher, William Kiester, for showing interest in my work and in my experiences—for making this book possible and giving me the opportunity to create this book and publish it, and for my recipes and stories to reach the world!

A big thank you to my editor, Sarah Monroe, for all the guidance throughout this whole process. All your comments, tips and suggestions didn't just help me improve my writing, but have also given me a better understanding of what it's like to properly relay a message for people to better understand and learn from. I still remember our first phone call when you helped me brainstorm on what it was I wanted to pursue, and that's led us to this point. I will forever be grateful for the chance to have worked on this book with you.

To my copyeditor, Iris Bass, for going through every single line of my manuscript and making sure even the tiniest details were clear, concise and easily understandable. Thank you for your time and patience in making sure everything is in tip-top shape.

To the design team, especially Meg Baskis, Kylie Alexander and Laura Benton, thank you for creating such a beautiful representation of my ideas and putting them into reality. I know I've provided countless versions of my cover for the team to mock up, so thank you for bearing with my indecisiveness.

I am extremely grateful to my parents: Thank you, Mommy and Daddy, for the love and guidance; for teaching me the importance of hard work early on; for exposing me to the world of travel and for opening my eyes and mind to different cultures that make us all unique. If it weren't for you and all the years you tirelessly worked to provide for me, I wouldn't have been able to pursue a path I was passionate about. I wouldn't have been in the position to share my recipes and write about my stories if it weren't for the both of you, whose sacrifices gave me these opportunities. I also express my love and gratitude to my Achi, my older sister, for bearing with my late nights and for always keeping me in check. Thank you for constantly reminding me to sleep and get some rest. You've witnessed me throughout my journey of starting out my blog all the way to years after when I've had the opportunity to write this book. You've also always given me constructive criticism and ideas on which recipes to do next and what I could improve on—and for that, I'm very thankful.

I also thank my best friends for believing in me from the beginning. You guys have always pushed me to do better and have remained my constant support system throughout. You have shown me all the love and support from the very beginning—from the early days when I was still navigating my way as a vegan in college—and were the guiding light on days when I doubted myself and my capabilities. Thank you for helping me believe in myself to pursue what it was that made me happy, no matter how hard. You've not only helped me grow as an individual, but have also taught me the importance of valuing those around me. Thank you for being my helping hands in the kitchen, being my taste testers and appreciating my food—whether good or bad!

My thanks and appreciation also go to all the people who have followed me on this journey. Thank you for giving my recipes a chance, trying them and sharing your feedback with me. I am and always will be grateful to have been able to connect with so many amazing individuals from all parts of the globe and to be able to share stories and experiences with you. It's from your stories that I also gain inspiration and drive. Whether you've been there since the beginning of The Foodie Takes Flight or have seen me at the latter parts where I've already started to spread my wings, thank you for helping me fly!

Last but not least, thank YOU. Thank you for giving this book a chance and for even making it as far as the end of the acknowledgments! Sending you lots of hugs.

Thank you, Maraming Salamat!

About the Author

Jessica Uy, better known as Jeeca, is an avid home cook, vegan recipe developer, food blogger and photographer behind The Foodie Takes Flight, a popular recipe blog and Instagram account. What started out as merely an account to document her day-to-day meals and food discoveries when she first switched to veganism eventually grew into a platform of hundreds of thousands where she shares vegan recipes inspired by the dishes she grew up enjoying and experienced from her travels. Her cooking is heavily influenced by her Chinese-Filipino upbringing that fuses together both East and Southeast Asian flavors. Her work has been featured on and published in Thrive Mags, Vegan Food and Living and the feedfeed, among others.

Index